ISLES OF SCILLY
FOLK
TALES

ISLES OF SCILLY
FOLK
TALES

MIKE O'CONNOR

The
History
Press

First published 2020

The History Press
97 St George's Place, Cheltenham,
Gloucestershire, GL50 3QB
www.thehistorypress.co.uk

British Library Cataloguing in Publication Data.
A catalogue record for this book is available from the British Library.

ISBN 978 0 7509 9078 3

Typesetting and origination by The History Press
Printed in Great Britain

CONTENTS

ADRO DHE'N AWTOUR

ABOUT THE AUTHOR

Mike O'Connor OBE is an expert in both the folklore and the ancient music of his home of Cornwall.

Mike is known for his work for the TV series *Poldark*, selecting and arranging the historical music and writing lovely songs for Demelza. But among folklorists he is known as a great storyteller and for his research of the world of travelling storytellers in Cornwall, a world described in his best-selling *Cornish Folktales* and *Cornish Folktales for Children* and revisited in this book.

Mike is a storyteller, fiddler and singer, as is Anthony James, one of this book's central figures. Sometimes writer and character are hard to separate!

When reading this book it's as if the reader, like the writer before, is travelling the lanes in the footsteps of Anthony and his son Jamie, swapping stories as the miles flow past.

RAGLAVAR

INTRODUCTION

This book tells tales from and about the Isles of Scilly and surrounds them with folklore, history and geography. Historical tales concerning the islands are up to 2,500 years old, saints' tales 1,500 years and literary romances 900 years.

Systematic recording of Cornish folk tales began in the nineteenth century. In 1851 Henry Whitfield, a Buckinghamshire parson staying in Penzance for his health, visited the Isles for three months and wrote *The Isles of Scilly and its Legends*. This was a pioneering enterprise, commendable in many ways. But Whitfield lacked the local knowledge and common touch of native writers. He wrote that 'popular superstitions' were few and attributed the lack of ancient material to cultural discontinuity. He commented:

> The whole population dates no farther back than from the days of
> Cromwell. It is entirely modern, having its tales of horror indeed, but
> relating only to smuggling, and wrecking, and disasters akin to them.
> The most remote of these dark scenes scarcely amounts up to a period
> of a hundred years ago.

So, whilst Whitfield did collect tales, with skill he also created fictional 'legends' of his own, for which he was later criticised in folkloric circles.*

---

* Folklorist M.A. Courtney wrote of Whitfield, 'his legends are for the most part
purely fictitious, and its title, Scilly and its Legends, a little misleading.'

But others did know local tales. Notable was Emma Jenkin Tiddy (1880–1962), a native of St Mary's and author of *Maze of Scilly*. She wrote that most of her tales were based on historical events. This prompts the question, when, if ever, does a historical narrative become a folk tale? On Scilly many factual events have lodged in community consciousness and have been retold many times, a folkloric process giving birth to variants and elaborations. Such tales include the St Agnes Tragedy, noted by Leland (*c*.1540), the Wreck of the Association (1707) and the Ghost of Rosevear (1784). Tiddy's tales date from 1707 to 1862. She was born in 1880 and it is probable that her stories were mainly orally transmitted. They show local knowledge and reflect tradition. History and folklore exist in parallel.

The tales in this book are told as the fictional travelogue of blind Anthony James, a travelling 'droll-teller', i.e. storyteller from Cury on the Lizard. Anthony, guided by his son Jamie, walked through Cornwall living on tales, songs and tunes. Like Anthony, most of the 'supporting cast' in this book are real. However, for reasons that will become apparent I have artificially placed both Robert Heath and Henry Whitfield in the book's early nineteenth-century timeframe.

It's easy to wander the islands imagining the way things were centuries ago. There is open ground where visitors can roam freely and there are well-signed lanes and paths. Scillonians are friendly and welcoming, but there is farmland and private property to be respected. The tides and currents are swift and can be hazardous. Take local advice on swimming; do not try to wade between the islands except under supervision. Respect the wildlife. Enjoy the knowledge and skill of the boatmen. Above all, let the atmosphere, the beauty and the history of the place wash over you, and enjoy its story.

PROLOGUE

It was a blissful spring morning on the island of St Mary's in the Isles of Scilly. The warm sun sparkled on the water and small boats bustled here and there. On a bench outside the Union Inn sat three storytellers.

There was Anthony James, a blind travelling droll-teller from Cury on the Lizard, his son Jamie, and Lizzie Tregarthen, the daughter of an old Scillonian sea captain. Lizzie wore a curious necklace made of irregular beads and hairy string.

'Lizzie,' said Anthony, 'We've a present for you.'

'Thank you,' cried Lizzie, unwrapping the parcel. Then she laughed with delight: inside was a book. The title was *Folk Tales of the Isles of Scilly* and the authors' names were Eliza Tregarthen, Anthony James and James Vingo James.

'That's me!' she screamed, 'But I didn't write anything.'

'You told most of the stories and you were a wonderful guide to the islands. This book tells how we came to the Isles of Scilly and all the adventures and stories we shared. Jamie wrote them down and I helped.'

As Lizzie looked at the book she fingered the beads of her necklace. A tear ran down her cheek. 'It's all the stories in my story necklace, they've come back to life.'

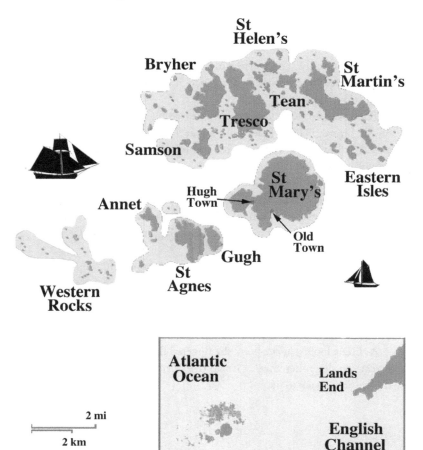

The Isles
of Scilly

St
Helen's

Bryher

St
Martin's

Tean

Tresco

Samson

Eastern
Isles

St
Mary's

Hugh
Town

Annet

Old
Town

Gugh

St
Agnes

Western
Rocks

2 mi

2 km

Atlantic
Ocean

Lands
End

English
Channel

1

ONAN

FLIGHT INTO
THE OCEAN

There's always room for a story that can transport people to another place.
J.K. Rowling

Anthony James and his son Jamie were tucking into stew in the snug of the Admiral Benbow Inn on Chapel Street in Penzance. With them was their friend Henny Quick who, as usual, was accompanied by a battered top hat and an expression of impending doom. For once he was not wrong.

The snug was dark; its old wooden panels were lit by just one candle. But outside the night was darker; the moon and the stars were masked by swift-moving clouds.

The Benbow was quiet. Earlier a tall young man had looked through the door. He gazed studiously at young Jamie's fiddle in its distinctive bag and then went on his way.

But now they heard footsteps outside. The door opened and an angry figure scowled at them. Instantly he was rebuked by Henny, 'Repent, for the hour of judgement is at hand!'

The figure cursed and vanished into the night.

Supper continued. Anthony, who was blind, ate steadily. Young Jamie, his guide and helper, wolfed down his food; it had been a day since their last meal.

Then from the darkness outside came shouts. A scuffle was taking place. Two burly figures appeared in the door.

'Down, under the table!' commanded a voice.

Anthony and Jamie ducked under the table. More figures crowded the doorway.

'They're not here,' said the voice. 'But there's two strong lads next door.'

Then came startled cries. Two figures were dragged from the next room into the darkness.

Jamie peered from under the table. A man in sea-boots appeared in the door. He grabbed Jamie and clamped his hand across Jamie's mouth. A blow to Jamie's head left him unconscious as he was dragged into the night.

In the inn, Henny Quick dolefully recited, 'Expect the dreadful day of doom! And a curse on the press gang!'

Beside him Anthony called out, 'Jamie, where are you?'

There was no reply.

Jamie came round in darkness. His head was sore and it felt as if the room was swaying. 'Anthony?' he cried, close to tears. There was no answer.

Jamie sat up and hit his head on the ceiling. He felt about him – he seemed to be in a triangular cupboard. He found a handle, turned it and pushed. The door opened suddenly and Jamie tumbled onto the floor. He picked himself up; though it was dark he realised he was in the fore-cabin of a small ship and the ship was under way.

Jamie tiptoed across the cabin and found a door leading aft. Beyond it a companionway led up to the deck. He climbed until he could peer out.

'You, get down!'

Jamie stumbled back down the steps. A tall figure followed him into the cabin. A familiar voice said, 'Dedh da, Jamie!*' It's best you stay out of sight.'

In the darkened cabin Jamie could not see who it was, but the voice was not threatening.

---

*   Good day, Jamie.

'Dedh da,' stuttered Jamie instinctively. 'Piw os ta? Who are you?'

'Myghtern Prussia ov vy!'

'Mr Carter!' Jamie breathed a sigh of relief.

John Carter, known locally as the King of Prussia, was captain of the *Phoenix*, a privateer sailing out of Prussia Cove. It was a ship well-known to excisemen, though none had ever proved its involvement in free trading.

'You're one of us,' said Carter. 'We couldn't let the press gang take you and leave Anthony with no guide. I'm sorry your head banged the door frame as we dragged you out.'

'Why don't the press gang take your men, Captain?'

'They are Sea Fencibles, volunteers sworn to defend the coast of Cornwall in the king's name. They can't be pressed any more than the constabulary.'

'What happened in the Benbow?'

'You and Anthony were seen by one of the mayor's cronies. You know Boase doesn't like you. His vendetta against Romanies and itinerants includes travelling droll-tellers. You've embarrassed him in public twice before. He'd love to see you pressed and Anthony stuck in Stoke Hospital, so he called in the press gang. You're going to have to lay low for a while. But at least for the moment he is distracted.'

'How's that?'

'My bosun spotted two trainee excisemen in the next bar. Right now they are in chains on the *Indefatigable* having been pressed! Tomorrow there will be an unholy row, they will have to be released and the mayor will get his knuckles rapped!'

Jamie laughed.

'But now I must take you where they can't find you.'

'Where are we going?'

'Enesek Syllan, the Isles of Scilly. Twenty-five miles of rough water beyond Land's End. But even there you must be careful. The Constable of Penzance is a vengeful man.'

'Mr Carter?'

'Yes, Jamie?'

'Please, where's my dad?'

There was an awkward silence.

WEATHERILL'S GHOST

At that moment a lookout called out, 'Bear away, bear away, the Runnell Stone, on the bow!'

The ship lurched as the *Phoenix* turned sharply to leeward. In the darkness Jamie could hear breakers. He sensed rough water on the starboard side.

'Well spotted, Mr Weatherill,' said John Carter.

'Thank 'ee, Cap'n,' said the helmsman. 'There's many a good ship gone down on the Runnell Stone,'

Weatherill declaimed into the night, as if his tale was a personal litany.

'Scillonians like me have always been mariners – how can we be anything else? We are born in the midst of the sea; we know its ways. But good fortune doesn't always attend even the best of us.

'Such a man was my cousin Richard Weatherill, cap'n of the brig *Aurora*. A good man, but he still went down to Davy Jones' locker. Have 'ee been to St Levan, boy?'

'Yes,' said Jamie, 'I saw the split stone in the churchyard and I know St Levan's prophecy:

'When with panniers astride,
A Pack Horse can ride,
Through St Levan's Stone,
The world will be done.'

'Good man! But mind you, don' go there at eight bells.'

'Why not?'

'All sailors on passage between Scilly and Mounts Bay have to pass the Runnell Stone, a mile south of Gwennap Head. One December night the *Aurora* was off West Penwith. Richard Weatherill was just about to sound eight bells, signifying the end of the watch. But his ship struck that rock and went straight to the bottom. He went down with his ship. But as it sank he was heard still sounding eight bells to mark the end of his watch on earth.

They buried him in St Levan churchyard. Not long after, some youngsters gathered there one Sunday morning. The service had started and the elders were in church. But the young folks were outside, chatting and passing the time, wandering among the graves, looking at the flowers and so on. When they came to Wetherill's tomb one girl paused to read the inscription. Suddenly she started in fright as she heard a hollow sound beneath her feet. The others saw her reaction and came close. They all heard it: a ringing sound, like a ship's bell. Terrified, they rushed into the church, interrupting the service. People talked about it for weeks after and there was no more gossiping in the churchyard on Sunday mornings.

'Soon after that a young sailor, originally from St Levan, came home on a visit after years away. He was in the Elder Tree one morning, chatting with friends. They mentioned the ship's bell in Wetherill's grave. The sailor said it was all nonsense. But, as it was nearly midday, for curiosity's sake, he went and listened by the captain's tomb; his friends stood by the church porch watching the sun dial. As it marked noon the sailor ran back to his friends, pale as a corpse, saying, "True as I'm alive, I heard eight bells struck in the grave. I'll not go there again for anything."

'That young man, on his very next voyage, went to a watery grave. So we know that if you stand on his grave at the right time you can hear Wetherill's ghost ringing eight bells down below, and if you hear that sound then you won't live out the year, you mark my words!

'We're a scary family,' said the old mariner, 'but you'll be thankful to know that I'm the last of 'em.'

LANDFALL

'When will we arrive?' asked Jamie.

'Tomorrow afternoon,' said Captain Carter. 'The wind is west-south-west, so we must beat all the way. It's 45 miles from Penzance to Scilly, but we will sail 90. You'll find blankets in the fore-peak. Get yourself some sleep.'

Next day Jamie was leaning on the rail. Ahead the islands rose from the sea and Jamie felt that lifting of the spirit that all sailors feel when they make landfall.

'That's St Mary's on the bow,' said John Carter. 'To the south that's St Agnes. To the north is St Martin's. Beyond are Tresco, Samson and Bryher. They are the islands that are inhabited."*

Soon the *Phoenix* was gliding into Old Town cove on St Mary's, the largest of the Isles of Scilly. Another craft was already at anchor: a single-masted lugger, the *Happy-Go-Lucky*.

Wetherill leaned on the rail beside Jamie. 'She's a shallop. Shallow draft, ideal for Scilly. Fast under sail, light enough to row. Mind you, she's darned uncomfortable in a seaway.'

A figure sat at the stern of the *Happy-Go-Lucky* nursing a blunderbuss. He studied the *Phoenix* for a moment and gave a wave of recognition. Wetherill waved back. Soon they were anchored, the dinghy was lowered and Jamie was rowed ashore. As they passed the *Happy-Go-Lucky* its lookout mysteriously called out, 'Try the Union', then went below.

The bow of the dinghy crunched into the gravel of Old Town Cove and Jamie jumped ashore. In his pocket was a pound note that John Carter had given him. As he looked back into the cove the *Phoenix* was already preparing for sea.

For a moment Jamie felt fear. He was alone, in a place quite unknown to him, and without his dad. Then he heard a kindly voice: 'You look proper mazed! Piskey-led I'd say.'

An ample lady had appeared from the cottages of Old Town. On her arm was a basket of provisions.

'Now then, boy,' she said, 'where are you goin'?'

Jamie's mind was blank. He didn't know where he was or where he was going. Then two words came to his mind.

'The Union.'

'I'll take you past Buzza Hill,' said the lady, 'then the way will be clear. Now then, what's your name?'

'Jamie.'

'Well mine is Mary Jenkin, but everyone calls me Aunt Polly, so you better do the same!'

*   Now only five are inhabited; Samson was evacuated in 1855.

As they passed Old Town church a clerical figure emerged, looked at them and snorted in displeasure.

As they walked along they chatted. Jamie realised that Aunt Polly's accent was not like his own. The 'th' at the beginning of words was rarely sounded. Thread was tread, pint was point, and point was pint.

Polly laughed, 'Each island has an accent of its own.'

In ten minutes they crested the hill.

'There you are,' said Aunt Polly. 'Just down there are the first houses. Now I'm away to see old widow Banfield.'

The cottages of Hugh Town were small, built of rough stone. The roofs were criss-crossed with straw rope to keep the thatch secure during gales. There seemed to be one of every trade: smith, carpenter, wheelwright, cooper, cobbler, tailor. Lady seamstresses worked in their doorways to get the best light. On the beach a ship was being built.

At the door of the Union Inn Jamie hesitated; he usually only visited such places with his dad. Gingerly he stepped inside; it was poorly lit. From the shadows a hand seized his shoulder.

'Come on,' said a gruff voice. 'You're expected.'

The speaker, an old shipmaster, propelled Jamie into a back room. From the gloom came a quiet voice, 'Jamie, what took you so long?'

It was Anthony James.

Father and son hugged each other with unrestrained joy. Then Captain Tregarthen, the shipmaster, introduced himself and his daughter Lizzie, who was about Jamie's age.

'Dad,' cried Jamie, 'how did you get here?'

'Same way as Jackey Treleaven. It was like this.'

JACKEY'S RIDE TO SCILLY

Jackey Treleaven was a good man, sober and honest. He must have been – he was a storyteller! He began all his stories by saying, 'I won't tell 'e a word of a lie *and know it*!' Mind you, those words are now an everyday saying when anything doubtful is related!

When Jackey was a lad he lived north of St Just and courted a maid who lived up at Tardinney with her folks. One Sunday afternoon he called on Mally, his sweetheart. Whilst she was out milking and he was keeping her company, her mam made a gurt currant cake so Jackey had a hearty meal. But then the old lady said, 'Jackey, as it's the first Sunday in May I've made you a junket.'

'Bless you,' said Jackey. 'But I'm so full I don't think I've got room.'

'Don't be silly,' said she. 'Go outside and jump up and down, shake your tea down a bit! Junket isn't filling.'

So Jackey went out and jumped up and down. When he came back, there on the table was a two-pint basin of junket, well-spread with thick cream and honey.

Whilst Jackey finished the junket, his sweetheart put on her Sunday best. Then down they went to Sennen Church-Town to the Methodist meeting with their friends. Preaching over, they all went into the First and Last for a drop of something sociable.

Now Santusters (people from St Just, that is) are always generous. Each of the ladies had a glass of gin-and-peppermint or brandy and cloves, or both if they liked, and a glass of shrub, too. The men had a few mugs of shenackrum* and a dram of rum to finish off.

Then it was time to go. They walked together to Burying-Place Downs. There the Santusters went Brea way, singing revival hymns as they went. But Jackey had to take his sweetheart back to Tardinney.

It was late when they arrived; the old folks were in bed, but the turf-fire still glowed, so they stayed courting till one in the morning. But before Jackey left, Mally gave him a modest supper of half a dozen boiled eggs. Jackey ate them with bread and butter, then he had a good piece of cake, left over from tea, and a bowl of milk. Then they kissed, said goodnight and Jackey started for home.

Poor Jackey had been on his feet most of the day and he still had nearly 4 miles to go. Halfway across Kelynack Downs he sat down to rest; he felt tired enough to sleep in a puddle! He wished he could find an old horse to ride – there were usually plenty grazing on the common.

He hadn't gone more than a hundred yards when his wish was granted. He saw an old black horse standing stock still, as if asleep, close by the

---

*   Shenackrum = gin and beer.

road, tied to a fence post with some hairy string. Jackey untied it and mounted it. Then he tried to direct it on the road home. But it took no notice of him and instead it took off westward over the downs, going slowly at first, but then getting faster and faster till it was galloping like the wind. It went so fast that Jackey had to hold on tight to avoid being blown off.

Soon they reached Land's End, but the horse did not hesitate; it leapt straight off the cliff. Jackey was sure he was going to die, but the horse did not plummet to the rocks below – it flew through the air. Soon it was skimming the sea towards the Isles of Scilly. Jackey could see St Agnes' light house.

After fifteen minutes they reached St Agnes but the horse did not pause. It went around and across and up so high that Jackey saw all the islands spread out like a map. He saw them so clearly that he remembered their positions ever after.

Then, without any direction from Jackey, the steed turned around and brought him back, about daybreak, to Kelynack Downs, just a stone's throw from where he started. Then the horse shook him off onto the ground and vanished in flames and smoke. It had been none other than the devil himself.

That's how the devil took Jackey to Scilly and back again. If anyone ever suggested to Jackey that his tale wasn't true or he fell asleep on Kelynack Downs and got hilla-rodden,* he would say. 'If you give me a piece of chalk I'll mark out all the islands as correct as anyone who lives there. Yet I had never been to Scilly before, nor have I since that night. Bless the Lord, I had a narrow escape. But I learned my lesson. To avoid staying up late courting, Mally and me got wed as soon as we could. Remember, I won't tell 'e a word of a lie *and know it*!'

---

* Got hilla-rodden: had a nightmare.

THE BRANDYMEN

Jamie laughed, 'Anthony, how did you really get here?'

'The Benbow is the chief smugglers' pub in Penzance. It's the base of Octavius Lanyon and the Benbow Brandymen.

'After John Carter saved you from the press gang, he knew the mayor would send his constable after me, and he did. Octavius climbed on the roof and fired his pistol to create a diversion while his lads took me to the kitchen of the Benbow. There's a secret tunnel leading to Abbey Slip. Normally it's used to bring up brandy and tobacco. They took me down it to the harbour and the *Happy-Go-Lucky*.

'Poor Octavius was wounded, but we managed to get away. Then, 2 miles off Penzance, we were spotted by the *Hawk,* the excise lugger. But the Brandymen escaped into the night by rowing directly into wind where the lugger couldn't sail.

'So now we are on the Isles of Scilly. John Carter will let Martha and Sarah know we are safe. We just have to earn a living until Boase's term as Justice of the Peace ends in November.'

'How do we do that?' asked Jamie.

'What we normally do: tell stories. The islanders are not rich but they are warm-hearted. They will enjoy our tales and we can learn some from them I'm sure.

'But we'd better leave Hugh Town for a while. There are men in authority here: army, excise, the constable, the parson. Some may be less sympathetic than others.'

Jamie looked at the sparkling water, the small boats going to and fro, and the islands basking in the sun.

'Scilly looks magical.'

'It is. But now we must rest. Tonight we begin our education with the oldest stories about the Isles of Scilly. We must be like sailors approaching the islands, feeling the first ripples they leave on the sea of history.'

2

DEW

THE NIGHT'S ARC OF STORIES

Tradition is not the worship of ashes, but the preservation of fire.
Gustav Mahler

The sun was on the western horizon. A golden pathway stretched across the sea and shadows lengthened. In the ocean the islands floated in a shimmering dream of light. Captain Tregarthen led them from a world of shadow up onto Buzza Hill. There a fire was burning; around it were logs and benches. The last light hovered over the land, gently welcoming the first stars. From the gathering darkness other figures appeared. Old and young, men and women, all were welcomed to the fireside.

Then came a quiet voice, 'As it says in the Good Book: in the beginning was the word!'

Then the stories began.

CREATION

First God created the heavens and the earth.

'Let there be light,' he said, and there was light, and so it was that he created day and night.

Then he saw the earth was without form, so the Spirit of God moved upon the face of the waters.

It was the greatest of works, forming firmaments and deeps and dry lands, and after the second day of labour the Lord was feeling a little weary. As he was carrying a great shovel-full of earth and rock to make Ireland, his attention was distracted. His grip on the shovel wavered and some little bits of rock fell from the shovel into the sea, and they formed the Isles of Scilly.

The Lord heard the splash and looked at the little group of islands and saw that it was good.

Eventually, when mankind got there, they also saw that it was good, so they stayed.

The proof of this tale is in the animals you find here. When St Patrick drove out all the snakes and venomous reptiles from Ireland, out of some ancient geographical sympathy those animals were also banished from Scilly. You won't find any poisonous snakes here at all, so it must be true.

Of course, the good Lord knew that unintentional island creation due to weariness was not desirable, so he decreed that on every seventh day we should no longer labour. So it is that we have the Isles of Scilly to thank for our day of rest. To this day it is a fine place to take your ease, and move as nature intended, with the rhythm of the tides and the stars.

THE ISLANDS

Long ago the island of Ennor was severed from Cornwall.

Then the ice grew strong and brought flint and stone to Ennor's northern shore.

But when the sun grew strong the ice retreated.

The sea carved a channel that took Agnes and Annet from their mother; they were the first of the children of Ennor.

Next, the sea reached out and held Ennor by the waist, leaving only a narrow causeway between north and south.

Finally, the sea drew his hand across Ennor and the water flowed where his fingers had traced. Sampson, Bryher, Tresco, St Helen, Teän, St Martin: these are the next of the children of Ennor.

Ennor, mother of the islands, was christened Mary after the mother of God.

To the west are the Western Rocks.

To the east are the Eastern Isles.

These are the Isles of Scilly.

THE ANCESTORS

We are children of the Islands.

We are people of the sea.

Our fathers were one with wind and wave.

They spoke the old tongue; we call it Cornish.

They fished and farmed, kept cattle and sheep.

They dug for flint, they found tin and lead.

They set up standing stones; they made labyrinths; they worshipped long-forgotten gods.

On hilltops and headlands they lie in tombs of stone.

On the moor are their workings. In the sea caves are the scars of their axes. Their blood still stains the ocean.

These are our ancestors.

THE TRAVELLERS

The first great travellers were the Phoenicians. Five hundred years before Christ they built biremes, ships with two banks of oars and a great square sail. They traded all over the Mediterranean and founded the city of Carthage, now in Tunisia.

In those days tin was rare and precious. There were tales of islands in the north where it could be found, but even the great Greek historian Herodotus was uncertain of their location or even their existence.

But at the other end of the Mediterranean, Carthaginian sailors had heard of the western islands, the Oestrymnides. There a proud-spirited tribe plied the tempestuous ocean in hide-covered boats and traded tin and lead. So the Phoenician admiral Himilco set out to find them.[*]

After four months at sea he succeeded. But the Greeks envied the Phoenicians; they too wanted tin. So they asked him about the voyage. But Himilco was a storyteller; he said this:

'Friends, we all want swords, shields and bright metalware so we must have bronze. To make bronze we need tin. But tin comes only from the tin islands, beyond the end of the earth.

'This is no voyage for mortals. The journey is long and the dangers are many. In truth the first to guide us to the Tin Island was none other than Melkarth, the god of the sea.

'One bright morning, while our people were still slumbering beneath the citadel, we made our oblations to Melkarth. Leaving the outer harbour of Carthage, we stayed inshore, using the land breeze to avoid the currents with which the gods keep mortals east of the Pillars of Hercules. But beyond the Pillars there is sea without end and the dangers are legion. Without Melkarth we would surely have failed.

'Beyond Gades[**] no breezes blow. To make progress, the oarsmen must have the strength of oxen.

'Even so, near Cape St Vincent, although the rowers worked mightily, the ship's motion ceased. I looked over the side. Seaweed completely encased the hull. We tried to cut it away but the ship was trapped. We could go neither forward nor backward. We would have starved to death in the midst of the ocean, but great Melkarth saw our peril and tore away the weed.

'North of Corunna great storms blew. The waves were as tall as the mast. We thought we would be overwhelmed, but Melkarth stilled the waves.

---

[*]   *Himilco* is a Latin rendering of the Phoenician name *Chimilkât*, which means 'my brother is Milkât' or Melkarth.

[**]   Cadiz

'Then, far to the north of finis terra, came mist like a cloak on the ocean. For days we saw not even the blades of our own oars. Our clothes were wet through. We shivered in the cold. But Melkarth sailed with us; he kept us on our course.

'Finally there were treacherous shallows with many sea monsters. Hidden sand bars blocked the way. But Melkarth subdued the creatures and guided us to the tin islands.

'But Melkarth is the patron of us Phoenician sailors. Only the brothers of Melkarth can make this voyage and return!'

Rufius Festus Avienus recorded this tale. Pliny the Elder knew it for he wrote that Midacritus was the first to bring tin from Cassiteris. Midacritus was his word for Melkarth.

THE SACRIFICE

The villa of Posidonius the geographer was high above the harbour of Rhodes. From there he would gaze on the wine-dark sea and remember his great voyages. One day he received a visitor, a young man of a Greek family from Asia Minor. His name was Strabo.

'Teacher,' said Strabo, 'what lies beyond the Pillars of Hercules?'

Posidonius closed his eyes, remembered the feel of the west wind in his hair, and began to speak. 'To the north is Iberia. Farther north, near Finis Terra, the end of the earth, there is the harbour of Corunna. But those who are bold can sail even further, beyond the end of the earth.

'North of Corunna lie the Cassiterides, the tin islands. There are ten of them, close together. One is naught but desert, but the others are inhabited.

'The men wear black cloaks, their tunics reach to their feet and are tied about the breast. They walk with staves. They tend cattle; most are just herdsmen. But they have a secret.'

'A secret?' said Strabo. 'What is their secret?'

'Stannum and plumbum, tin and lead. They barter them for pottery, salt, and bronze vessels.

'But it is so far to sail, so dangerous …'

'But the world demands tin! Most of the tin in Europe comes from the Cassiterides. They say that the bronze in Solomon's temple was made from such tin.'

'Miraculum miraculorum esse, miracle of miracles!'

'Only the Phoenicians knew the way to the Cassiterides. The trade was so valuable that they would tell no one else. They just said that the god of the sea guided them.'

'Surely someone else could find out, the Romans?'

'The Romans! They want to conquer the world! Yes, they too were jealous of the Phoenicians so they sent one of their vessels to follow a Phoenician ship and find the route.

'When the Phoenician captain saw he was being followed, he guessed they were trying to discover the secret. He let the Roman ship get closer and closer. The Romans were so excited they did not pay attention to the hazards of the ocean.

'The Phoenician sea captain deliberately sailed his ship into the Western Rocks of Scilly and ran his ship onto a shoal. The Romans blindly followed him, only realising the danger when it was too late. The Roman ship struck the rocks and sank to the bottom of the sea.

'But the Phoenicians carried a dinghy for landing in shallow harbours. They used it as a lifeboat and were saved. So the Phoenicians kept their secret. For his brave deed the captain was rewarded with another ship by the Phoenician treasury.

'In time the Phoenician empire faded and the Romans did find the way. On the leeward side of Ennor they built a harbour and above it grew a village called Nornour.

'There they left coins, beads, brooches, bracelets and pottery. With them was the figurine of a goddess. Above the harbour was a shrine dedicated to a goddess. Some say she was Sillina, goddess of the Isles of Scilly.'

ICTIS

Strabo's tales inspired the Sicilian Diodorus. He wrote this:

> They that inhabit the British promontory of Belerion … prepare the tin, which … they dig out of the ground … they melt the metal and refine it. Then they cast it into regular blocks and carry it to a certain island near at hand called Ictis for at low tide, all being dry between there and the island, tin in large quantities is brought over in carts.

Where was Ictis? Scholars have suggested Looe Island, St Michael's Mount, the Mount Batten peninsula or even the Isle of Wight.

The Isle of Wight was far from the tin of Cornwall. The sea level was then lower so Mount Batten was high and dry and St Michael's Mount was in a swampy forest far from the sea. Looe Island had no links with the tin trade.

On the other hand, as the waters rose, the island of Ennor began to fragment. The northern islands were all linked by intertidal flats. Monks from Tresco processed to St Helen's on a tidal causeway. The only way the islanders could have accessed the port of Nornour is on such a causeway. The Isles of Scilly are a prime candidate for Ictis.

LYONESSE

In antiquity writers wrote of the Tin Island, the Island of Scilly: singular not plural. Inundation and fragmentation came later.

The legends of Lyonesse (Cornwall), Ys (Brittany) and Cantre'r Gwaelod (Wales) all suggest that the greatest flood came after the time of King Arthur and before the time of the Welsh bard Taliesin: perhaps the mid-sixth century.

Triads and other early Welsh manuscripts tell us that tales of Tristan were told in early Celtic oral tradition. In the twelfth century the tales were given literary form by writers such as Thomas of Britain and Beroul the Norman. Tristan was raised in Lyonesse, a land near Cornwall. He was abducted by pirates – a familiar occurrence on the Isles of Scilly.

This tradition was echoed by writers from Thomas Malory onwards. He mentioned Surluse, a part of Lyonesse where Sir Galahad ruled under Arthur.

LETHOWSOW

Inundation dominates the experience, landscape and folklore of the Isles of Scilly.

Some enjoy those inundation tales as mythology or literary invention. But they have a firm foundation.

The *Anglo-Saxon Chronicle* records many floods in the west. One such great flood was on St Martin's Day: 11 November 1099. They continue to this day.

On 26 September 1744: 'the Sea rolled in vast Mountains, driven by the Winds, and broke over the Banks of Percressa, next the Southward, where it entered the Town (Hugh Town) with such Violence and Rapidity, as threatened the levelling of all the Houses'. The storm also damaged Old Town and flooded the Lower Moors.

On 1 November 1755, after the Lisbon earthquake, three great waves swept over Scilly with 'great loss of life and property'.

In 1771 yet another storm broke through from Porthcressa and flooded Hugh Town.

Flood tales are alive in the islands' consciousness.

Off our coasts are submerged forests and peat beds. The old Cornish name for St Michael's Mount is Carrack Looz en Cooz: the grey rock in the wood.

At the lowest tides we walk from Tresco to Samson and Bryher. We see the old field boundaries and hut circles on the tidal flats around the islands.

Below high water on Old Man, west of Teän, is a stone grave with pottery and jewellery. Below high water on Nornour are the remains of a harbour. Both are from Roman times.

Scilly has not been linked to Cornwall for millennia, but evidence of submerged lands is all around.

Written accounts, oral testimony and archaeology have the same message. Our flood legends have truth within them as deep as the ocean.

We islanders know of Lyonesse, but we have our own tradition that stems from the inundation of the islands, first noted by William of Worcester in 1473.

The Cornish name for the land lost beneath the waves is Lethowsow: The Milky Ones. It's what fishermen called rocks such as the Seven Stones Reef, where the white water endlessly breaks.

Lethowsow had 140 parishes with fine churches, woods and meadows, fertile fields all fringed with tamarisk. There was a watchtower at the western-most point. The chief town was called the City of Lions and there, long ago, lived a boy prince called Tristan. But day by day the sea grew bolder. Every month at spring tides the ocean spread its salty fingers over the fields: tentatively at first, but bolder with every full moon.

The first to notice was a man called Trevilian. He was alarmed by the daily advance of the sea, so he wisely sent his wife and family to safety in the hills of Cornwall. Then when the highest tide of the year came, when the full moon of the equinox shone on the first Autumnal gales, the waters rushed across the fields as never before. Trevilian leapt onto his horse – he had no time to saddle it – and rode bareback ahead of the flood. The waves were getting closer and closer, but he reached the high ground at Perranuthnoe, east of Penzance, just before they could engulf him. That is why the coat of arms of Trevelyan depicts a horse, without a saddle, emerging from the sea.

The governor of Lethowsow was called Vyvyan. He had a white horse ready saddled and bridled in his stable. He too galloped ahead of the waves. But his steed did not have the stamina of Trevillian's horse. The sea grew closer and closer and looked sure to engulf him. But at the last second the horse gathered all its strength and made a great leap. It landed at Trelowarren on the Lizard and there the Vyvyan family built a new house. So that is why the Vyvian shield is surmounted by a white horse, fully bridled, with one foot over the waves.

The Lord of Ganilly realised he could not ride the 25 miles to Sennen before the waters covered the land. He made his way to the harbour of Nornour and sheltered there until the harbour itself was inundated. Then he set out in a boat. Its high bow and stern protected him from the heavy seas. Its strong hull was made of precious oak and its sail was of leather, so it could stand up to the violent winds. Its flat bottom let him sail across the shallow waters. He landed safely at Sennen and there founded a chapel in thanks for his deliverance. It was called Chapel Idne, the narrow chapel. Sennen Cove was for years called Porth Gone Hollye: 'the port serving Ganilly'. Chapel Idne fell into disrepair as late as the sixteenth century.

There must have been other survivors: those who ran to the hills we now call islands, or who escaped in coracles or curraghs. But because the tales tell of 'sole survivors' it's clear that many were lost and the flooding of Lethowsow left a scar on the memory of the land.

Our fishermen declare that on still days and moonlit nights they see churches and houses under the water. The hill on which stood the city of Lions is the Seven Stones reef. Fishermen call it 'Tregva' or 'The Town'. There, in their nets they find domestic items and diamond-shaped panes set in lead, forming casements.

Lethowsow is shown on Mercator's chart of 1595 as 'uncovered at low tide'.

On quiet nights the bells of the churches can still be heard ringing beneath the waves. Where once were 140 parishes there are now 140 islands and 140 stories. Like the tales that surround them, the Isles of Scilly are a place where myth and history meet.

As the last tale ended, the first light appeared in the east. It was the time when night and day meet, and the stories and their tellers returned to their beds. As Anthony and Jamie pondered where they might go, a kindly man who seemed to be in charge gently placed his hand on Anthony's shoulder.

'Friends,' he said, 'you could rest in Mill Cottage if you wished.'

'Would the miller object?'

'It's the miller that invites you. Follow me.'

MAYBEE THE MILLER[*]

As they headed south, the miller introduced himself. 'My name is William Maybee.'

'Anthony James, and my son Jamie.'

On the headland was the windmill. A cottage was close by.

'Peninnis,' said Maybee.

'The head of the island,' translated Anthony. 'Does anyone speak Cornish here?'

'The fishermen have words of Cornish and most coastal features and rocks have Cornish names. But since the Civil War most people speak English.'

At Mill Cottage they were greeted by Florence, the miller's wife.

'Florrie Mumford I was. But now I'm Mrs Maybee and he's Mr Maybee, and we're both sure of it. But it was very tricky when we got married. For the parson my William 'ad to say, "I William maybe take thee Florence Mumford to be my lawful wedded wife." I 'ad to say, "I Florence Mumford take thee William maybe to be my lawful wedded husband." So I told the parson, "There's no maybe about it, there's no stopping us now!"'

They were still laughing when there was a knock at the door. It was Lizzie, the shipmaster's daughter.

'Breakfast!' she cried, producing five pilchards from her satchel.

With swift dexterity, Florrie gutted the fish and soon they were baking on a stone in the fire. Then she made flatbreads from a handful of flour. They ate their breakfast and then, as the sun grew higher, they found themselves dreaming of ancient sailors, lost lands, and church bells forever sounding beneath the waves.

---

[*]   William and Florence's son, Robert Maybee (1810–91), was a noted local 'folk poet'.

3

TREI

THE MILL OF HISTORY

If history were taught in the form of stories it would never be forgotten.
Rudyard Kipling

Peninnis Mill spread its sails towards the stars, as if to catch errant stories on the wind. On the ground floor benches lined the wall. A central pillar supported the floors above. A ladder climbed into the blackness.

'Welcome,' said Maybee the miller.

'Why have we come here?' asked Jamie.

Maybee smiled, 'Last night's tales came from ancient times when these islands were beyond the bounds of the known world, beyond the realms of kings and empires. Traders came under the sufferance of the gods of the ocean and there were no claims on the Isles of Scilly.

'But as the sea rose so did man's ideas of territory and power. Tonight's tales are from when the world began to impose on the islands. They set the scene for all that follows.

'Sounds grand, doesn't it? Then again,' he said with a wink, 'it's much warmer in here!'

The rest of the company gathered and the stories began.

KINGS AND PRINCES

After the Romans left in the year 410, Saxons came to Wessex. Over five centuries the Celts were pushed west through Somerset and Devon. William of Malmesbury wrote of the Saxon King Æthelstan:

> In 926 he turned towards the Western Britons, who are called the Cornwallish ... Fiercely attacking, he obliged them to retreat from Exeter, which, till that time, they had inhabited with equal privileges with the Angles, fixing the boundary of their province on the other side of the river Tamar ... This city then, which he had cleansed by purging it of its contaminated race, he fortified with towers and surrounded with a wall of squared stone.

The Cornish had to stay west of the Tamar, but King Æthelstan could go where he liked. In 931 he visited St Burian where he had already founded an oratory. Then he sailed to the Isles of Scilly. We don't know why. The tin was worked out and the Cornish-speaking population of subsistence farmers and fishermen was tiny. Scilly was remote, poor and a low priority for taxation, investment or defence. Æthelstan was probably asserting political influence at a time when the Cornish nobles were vulnerable.

After the Norman conquest the Isles of Scilly became part of the Earldom of Cornwall granted by William the Conqueror to his brother Robert, Earl of Mortain. But the Domesday Book does not mention Scilly – it was still too poor to tax.

However, by the late twelfth century the Isles had become feudally significant, 'appurtenant and owing allegiance to the honour of the Castle of Launceston'. A castle of Sullia is mentioned in 1194; Ennor Castle is named in a deed of 1244.

Edward I made Ranulph de Blanchminster* constable of the islands and its castle of Ennor in return for providing twelve men-at-arms to maintain the peace and the payment of an annual tribute. The small number of

---

*   aka Randolph de Blancheminster.

soldiers suggests that keeping order was not a major task. His rent or 'waiternfee', payable at the gate of Launceston Castle, was 'at the feast of St Michael the Archangel, 300 birds, called poffins, or 6s. 8d'.

Edward II granted a licence to crenellate Ennor Castle in 1315, which suggests increasing danger. Then in 1337 the castle, with the rest of Scilly, became part of the newly created Duchy of Cornwall. It was maintained until the sixteenth century.

SEA KINGS AND SALEEMEN

The isolation of the Isles left them vulnerable. In medieval times Vikings, here called Sea Kings, plundered the coasts. The Orkneyinga Saga describes a twelfth-century raid. Sweyn Asleifsson 'went south, under Ireland, and seized a barge belonging to some monks in Syllingar and plundered it. ... Three chiefs, Swein, Þorbjörn and Eirik, went ... to the Syllingar, where they gained a great victory in Maríuhöfn* on Columba's-mass and took much booty.'

But the outcome of such raids was not foregone. In 1209 the annals of Tavistock Abbey record the beheading of 112 pirates on the Island of St Nicholas, i.e. Tresco. As there were probably no more than twelve monks in the monastery and the Ennor garrison was about the same, it's hard to imagine the circumstances of this slaughter.

In 1342, 600 Welshmen 'were drawn by the sea on to that island, staying there for 20 days and carrying away £500 worth of crops'. Mercenaries becalmed en route to Brittany, they starved the outnumbered islanders.

In 1351 the monks on Tresco complained that pirates had destroyed most of their property.

In 1540 Leyland wrote: 'Few men be glad to inhabit these islets ... for Robbers by the Sea that take their Catail of Force. These Robbers be French Men and Spaniardes.'

Even after Star Castle was built, the Islands were vulnerable. In 1625 there were thirty Saleemen, Barbary pirate ships, off Scilly, and a year

---

*   *Þorbjörn*: Fairbairn. *Maríuhöfn*: Mary's Haven. Columba's mass is 9 June.

later Scilly was taken by Flemish privateers. During the First Anglo–Dutch War* the Scilly packet boat was captured by a Dutch warship. In 1677, during the third such war, Dutch sailors stole Scillonian sheep.

For all the posturing of English kings from Æthelstan to Charles II, the islands' isolation made them a tempting target.

WRECKERS

Wrecks, flotsam and jetsam were once vital to the Isles. The cargo and every part of a wrecked ship would be salvaged if possible. Most large timbers on the islands are from ships.

Reginald, Earl of Cornwall 1141–75, granted the monks of Scilly 'all wrecks, except whole ships and whales'. After the Reformation this right reverted to the Crown. By law all such items were supposed to be handed to the authorities, but this was not enforceable in such a remote community.

In 1305 a ship was wrecked on Tresco. A mob of wreckers was led by Randulph de Blanchminster, governor of the islands. When William le Poer, the coroner of Cornwall, tried to take charge of the cargo, he was imprisoned by Randulph until he was able to buy his freedom! On his release, le Poer petitioned Edward I. As a result, Scilly was given its own coroner, doubtless more amenable to the Blanchminsters.

Contrary to popular fiction, deliberately causing wrecks was impractical and unnecessary. False lights meant little in the days before lighthouses. Candle lanterns on the shore could not be seen at any distance. By the seventeenth century increasing sea trade meant more wrecks anyway. In 1680 the keeper of the newly built St Agnes lighthouse was accused of failing to light his fire until a ship, the *Golden Lion*, was wrecked and looted. However, the report was wildly inaccurate and the keeper was found not guilty.

The island of St Agnes was downwind of the notorious Western Rocks, so inevitably its people gained a bad reputation. But wrecking was central to all Scillonian life and even the clergy were involved.

*   1652–54.

The Wreckers' Prayer, 'We pray thee, O Lord, not that wrecks should happen, but if wrecks do happen Thou wilt guide them into the Scilly Isles for the benefit of the poor inhabitants!' is attributed to Rev. John Troutbeck, chaplain of the islands, 1780–96.

The position of the clergy is confirmed by the tale of a man bursting into a Cornish church one Sunday shouting, 'Wreck! Wreck!' The priest swiftly barred the door to stop his flock rushing to the shore – while he removed his robes.

'So we can all start fair,' he said!

PIRATES

The Isles of Scilly were notorious as a base for pirates.

In 1546, a pirate from Calais called Thomessin took control of the Isles in order to raid passing shipping. Thomas Seymour, the Lord High Admiral, was sent to remove him, but instead he did a deal and the two men shared both control of the islands and the profits. However, in 1549 both men were caught and executed. On learning of Seymour's demise, Princess Elizabeth remarked, 'This day died a man with much wit and very little judgment.'

That year Sir William Godolphin, Member of Parliament and High Sheriff of Cornwall, was made Governor of Scilly. But in this unassailable position he became known as 'Captain of the Group', ruling the pirates operating from the islands. On his death in 1571 Queen Elizabeth reasserted control, leasing the islands to Sir Francis Godolphin for a yearly rent of £10 on the condition he defended them. But after his governorship ended in 1608, pirates returned in the guise of privateers. They caused such mayhem that some called Scilly 'the second Algiers'.

THE KING'S PIRATE

John Mucknell was a captain of the British East India Company. In 1643 he was given command of the *John*, a new vessel: light, fast and with forty-four guns. He had orders to sail to Surat in India for a cargo of spices and silks. He was also tasked to collect a wealthy Portuguese ambassador en route. But the Civil War had then begun. Mucknell, a Royalist, decided to steal the ship.

At sea, Mucknell encouraged drunken fights so he could see which of his crew were loyal to the Company and which would side with him. Then he gave accompanying ships the slip and marooned both passengers and dissenting crewmen on the isle of Johanna near Mozambique. He sailed to Bristol, collected his wife and headed to the Scillies.

There Mucknell found a ragbag fleet of nine ships, many with dubious histories, and declared himself leader of this Royalist 'navy'. The Prince of Wales appointed him vice admiral and gave him a knighthood. Mucknell was authorised to attack Cromwell's ships and those of any country supporting Parliament. For five years Mucknell plundered ships of his old company and any foreign vessels that came close, including many Dutch ships.

In late 1646, Cromwell's men claimed the Scillies and the Royalist fleet fled the islands. But in 1648 Mucknell gained a powerful ally, Prince Rupert of the Rhine, a nephew of Charles I. Rupert brought eleven more ships and was put in charge of the combined fleet. In Kinsale they loaded Irish troops. The Isles of Scilly were retaken and the King appointed Sir John Grenville Governor of the Islands.

Once again Mucknell caused maritime mayhem. Cromwell's Admiral Blake wished 'that God or the gallows make an end of him'. Eventually, in 1651 Blake retook the Scillies. The Royalist fleet, now poorly maintained, was driven from the Channel. Off the Azores they encountered a great storm. On 30 September, Rupert's flagship *The Constant Reformation* sprang a huge leak and sank, taking 300 souls with it.

The Prince and his advisers survived but thereafter there is no news of John Mucknell. It seems he was drowned, but some like to think that he escaped to run a waterside inn in Wexford or Kinsale, where he could watch the tides and relive his eight years as both pirate king and King's Pirate.

THE CIVIL WAR

The Civil War began in 1642 though Scilly, traditionally Royalist, was not involved until February 1646, when the Prince of Wales, then only 15, fled from Falmouth to St Mary's and stayed for six weeks before continuing to Jersey.

St Michael's Mount fell in July that year, Pendennis Castle in August. In September, Scilly was claimed by Parliament. But in 1648 John Mucknell arrived and the islands declared for the king. Charles II made Sir John Grenville governor. He strengthened Star Castle and King Charles' Castle on Tresco.

Mucknell's privateers caused chaos at sea. Dutch losses were such that they sent a squadron of warships under Admiral Maarten Tromp. On 30 March 1651, he arrived off Scilly demanding the return of Dutch ships, crews and cargoes.

Cromwell's council ordered their 'General at Sea' Robert Blake and Sir George Ayscue to take on Grenville and, if necessary, Tromp. They sailed from Plymouth on 12 April with twenty-two ships and nine companies of troops.

Grenville released his Dutch prisoners to Tromp but the ships and cargoes were already sold. Grenville was confrontational and antagonistic so when Blake arrived Tromp offered to assist. Blake agreed a joint show of strength, but insisted that only English troops should invade the islands.

St Mary's was well defended so Blake decided to secure Tresco first. He attacked New Grimsby but was repulsed. Bad weather delayed the next assault until 17 April. That attack met rough seas, strong currents and robust opposition, ending up on the islands of Northwhethel and Teän. However, the next day a third attack, on Old Grimsby, was successful. Grenville's men fled to St Mary's.

Blake invited Grenville to surrender. On 2 May their deputies met on Samson but could not agree terms. So Blake built a gun position on the southern tip of Tresco. His warships joined in and St Mary's was constantly bombarded.

With no hope of relief Royalist morale faded. In mid-May Blake offered Grenville lenient terms. He surrendered and on 3 June 1651 Commonwealth troops garrisoned St Mary's. So fell the last Royalist stronghold in England.

CROMWELL'S TANKARD

Between 1651 and 1652, to guard New Grimsby, Blake built a new fort on Tresco, just south of King Charles' castle. Known as Cromwell's Castle, some believe Cromwell himself visited it. A large china tankard, from which he was said to have drunk his breakfast beer, exists to this very day.

The islanders had to accept whichever military master controlled their destiny. But at heart they were royalist. This verse was related by a Scillonian:

In Cromwell's days I was for him,
But now, my boys, I'm for the King;
For I can turn, boys, with the tide,
And wear my coat on the strongest side.

The modern age had arrived.

ST MARY'S

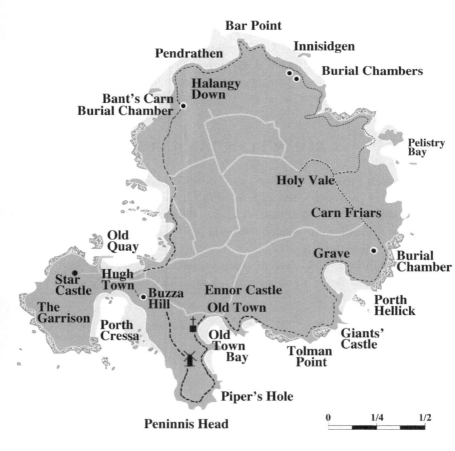

Bar Point

Pendrathen

Innisidgen

Burial Chambers

Halangy
Down

Bant's Carn
Burial Chamber

Pelistry
Bay

Holy Vale

Carn Friars

Old
Quay

Grave

Burial
Chamber

Star
Castle

Hugh
Town

Buzza
Hill

Ennor Castle

The
Garrison

Old Town

Porth
Hellick

Porth
Cressa

Old
Town
Bay

Giants'
Castle

Tolman
Point

Piper's Hole

Peninnis Head

0   1/4   1/2

4

PAJAR

ST MARY'S

St Mary's is the gateway. There you can choose to remain in the present,
but the past is only a few steps away.

After a morning's rest they stepped out onto Peninnis. It was time to
explore St Mary's.

Mr Maybee had a twinkle in his eye as they walked out onto the
headland. Then, from beneath their feet came an unearthly sound,
somewhere between a laugh and a hollow gurgle.

Jamie shivered in alarm.

'That,' said Mr Maybee, 'is Izzicumpucca! The name means this is
the hollow of Bucca, the legendary Cornish sea monster. He lives in
this cave right beneath our feet.'

IZZICUMPUCCA

The Sea Bucca is respected but always avoided by fishermen. They
suspect he can bring them bad luck if they annoy him, so they always
leave him something on the beach when they bring home their catch,
and in return he makes sure they always catch enough fish to eat.

The Bucca is dark and brown, with skin like a conger eel, and
tangled seaweed for hair. He is very lonely, and has a sad expression
on his face, like a hungry seal. Nobody goes near him except naughty

children, and even they are usually frightened away by his strange looks, though he is really very gentle and would love to talk to them.

He has not always been a Bucca. Many years ago he was human; he was a prince. He loved a young maiden, but she did not love him and she entered a convent just to avoid him. The prince was desolate, so he went to see a witch. For three gold pieces she cast a spell and turned him into a pigeon. He flew to the convent, found his love's cell and hopped in the window. Every day he returned. She loved the friendly little bird and would nurse it in her bosom.

But one day a monk, who came to the convent to hear confessions, found her with the pigeon. Although the nuns lived only on bread and water, in the company of the pigeon she had grown more lovely and contented than ever; her cheeks bloomed like roses, unlike those of the other nuns.

The monk guessed that the pigeon was the reason she had blossomed, so by magic he undid the spell and the pigeon turned back into a prince. Immediately the maiden fell in love with the prince and would have run away with him. But before they could flee, the monk put a curse on him and turned him into a Sea Bucca for a thousand years, unless he could win another woman's love to set him free.

So there, swimming in the waves, lying in the sea caverns, or sitting on the rocks with the birds, was Bucca. As long as the fishermen did him no harm he helped them, driving fish into their nets and filling their crab and lobster pots. Then one day old Uncle Malachi took his little grand-daughter Grace in the boat with him. Alas, she leaned over the side too far and fell overboard. But Bucca held up the child, so that Uncle Malachi could lift her safely back on board. From then on Bucca made sure that each time Grace went to sea with her grandad, the old man caught fish after fish and had enough to spare. 'Malachi's luck' they called it.

In time the little girl grew into a young woman. Bucca hoped that she might grow to love him, but she had many admirers on land, and finally she gave her heart to a lad called Seth.

After they were married she would sit outside their cottage, mending his net and baiting his lines, but she never went to sea because Seth, like everyone else, thought it was bad luck to have a married woman aboard a ship.

One evening when Seth was at sea, Grace was sighing at having so much work to do, when a voice said, 'Don't 'ee fret, my dear – I'll help 'ee.'

It was Bucca, and in a few minutes he had mended the net and baited the hooks. After that, whenever Seth wasn't there, he came and helped Grace, or told her wonderful stories of a handsome prince, though she only laughed at him for being 'so soft', as she called it. It was useless her telling him not to come, for he could change into a seagull, or even become invisible. Often he was there when she didn't know it, filling her mind with tales of a handsome prince who loved her. Grace never suspected that Bucca was really the prince.

Then one night Grace had the most vivid dream. In it her prince lover touched her lips and whispered softly. She rose in her sleep and followed the vision. She untied Seth's boat and took the oars. But Bucca was there. He lifted their weight and drew back the waves so that the boat travelled swiftly and Grace still slept. When the boat was far from land her dream changed and the prince became Bucca, who knelt before her, his sea locks dripping, imploring for a woman's love to restore him to his human state.

There was pity in her soul. The fishes swam round the boat to witness the strange courtship, wondering what would happen. The night was dark and the stars jewelled the sky and sea. Grace, under the enchantment of a spell, lifted Bucca's head and looked into his eyes. But they were dull, they were not lit with the light of the eyes of men.

Then suddenly the boat lurched. Grace woke and right in front of her was Bucca, with his great big fishy eyes, his cold wet conger eel body and dripping seaweed hair. She screamed in terror.

In the cove, Seth heard the scream and saw the little boat on the horizon. Then he saw it turn and surge towards the land, as if propelled by some invisible power.

As the keel crunched on the gravel Seth saw Bucca leave the stern and swim out to sea. He called and thanked Bucca for rescuing Grace. He thought she had been sleepwalking and she never told anyone but me what really happened.

That was the nearest Bucca ever got to winning his love. He still swims out there and helps to fill crab pots and nets. But no girl or woman ever goes to sea, for now they know how he lured Grace that night.

Bucca must wait another hundred years before he changes back into a prince. Unless, of course, a maiden that is bolder than usual hears this tale, and rows out to look for him, and then ... who knows?

In the meantime, just remember that the gurgling sound you hear on Peninnis is really Bucca laughing to himself as he anticipates coming from his cave to look for his lunch.

THE TALE OF PIPER'S HOLE

Not far from Izzicumpucca is the cave called Piper's Hole. Its mouth is almost high enough for a man to stand, but inside it gets narrower and lower. Water constantly falls from the roof and runs down the walls into rock basins, which overflow to create a pool of fresh water. Beyond it the cavern extends further, but no one knows how far, for no one who has gone further has ever returned.

Old folks tell tales about the cave: of men stuck and unable to retreat, lost in a labyrinth, fallen over a precipice, drowned in a pool, caught by a ghost, or even eaten by a monster.

Some say that the cavern is linked with another of the same name on Tresco. They tell of dogs that went in one end and emerged at the other days later, thin and hungry and with most of their hair scraped off, so narrow is the passage.

The story goes that one night old Ellis the piper played late at the inn. He played so late he missed the boat to Tresco, and then the water was too low to sail, too high to wade and too far to swim. But he had to be back at work on the farm first thing the next day.

Said Ellis, 'I shall walk home through the Piper's Hole.'

His friends begged him not to go, but he was insistent.

He said, 'I'll play my pipes as I go, and as long as you can hear them you'll know that I'm all right.'

Then he set off down the tunnel. His friends heard the pipes growing fainter and fainter until they were heard no more.

Next morning they sailed across to Tresco and asked at the farm. Ellis was not there. They went to the north of the island and scrambled down to the cave. They went as far as they dared and listened carefully.

Some said they could hear pipes faintly playing in the distance; others said they were imagining things. They waited all day, and the next, but Ellis was never seen again.

No one has ever tried to follow him. But if you go down to the cave on a quiet night you can still sometimes hear the sound of pipes playing, far, far beneath the ground.

PITT'S WAGER

The view from Peninnis was magnificent. William Maybee pointed out the Giants' Castle to the east, Agnes to the south and the Garrison to the west.

'There are some fine rock shelters and grassy hollows from which you can enjoy these views. Over there is Sleep's Abode and just there is Pitt's Parlour, where that rascally Pitt used to meet his friends and paramours.

'Not too long ago the Governor of the Isles was George Osborne, Duke of Leeds. He was very proud of the islands and the islanders. He took every opportunity to praise the place, its honest men and its virtuous women. But it so happened that once on a visit to London he met a young man called Thomas Pitt, a distant cousin of the prime minister.

'Now Pitt was a rake and a hellraiser and the first thing he did was challenge young Osborne, who not only repeated his claims about the Isles of Scilly, but then went further. He was prepared to wager that such was the virtue of the ladies of Scilly that not a single wayward soul could be found among them. Inevitably Pitt took up the bet and rashly wagered his family fortune that he would, within a month, prove that Osborne's claim was false. And a very great fortune it was, for his family's wealth was based on the famous Pitt diamond, worth millions of pounds.

'So, Pitt travelled down to Scilly to find a lady to inveigle and so save his family fortune. Pitt's Parlour was his favourite trysting place. There he would whisper lie after lie, trying to lead astray the young ladies of Scilly. He bought them fine meals, fine wine and expensive gifts.

But they could see right through him, every one. I'm told that more'n one of them deliberately led him on, just for what they could get out of him. Pitt got nowhere. As the days passed he became desperate, as it looked more and more certain that he was going to ruin himself by his bragging and his cavalier wager.

'Alas for the ladies of Scilly! Eventually one very poor girl was found who in return for a very large bribe was persuaded to save Thomas Pitt's family fortune! But though he was undoubtedly a cad and a bounder, in gratitude, he gave her a small pension for the rest of her days.'

'How did she save his fortune?' asked Jamie.

'I expect she gave him a big kiss,' said Lizzie.

THE GHOSTS OF LOST SHIPS

'I can tell you a story,' said Lizzie. 'An' I know it's true. My Gran says that if the victims of some awful crime can't rest in peace their ghosts return to the scene of their sufferings. The same is true of the perpetrators. If you see them it can reveal terrible secrets of the past.

'Back in the days of wrecking and pirates and such like, many evil deeds were done.

'About sixty years ago, a merchantman was captured by pirates and no one knew what happened to the crew or passengers. Afterwards, the ship was recaptured by the Royal Navy and brought here. All the pirates were locked up and the unmanned ship was moored alongside the quay.

'But as she lay there an inquisitive youth from Hugh Town crept on board. He peered through a crack in the partition and saw what seemed a kind of hen coop, newly painted green, just big enough to put two people in. Guarding it was a gentleman dressed in a dark suit with high boots, a lace collar, and a tricorn hat.

'The lad looked long and hard, to make sure of what he was seeing. Then he ran ashore and asked if anyone knew anything about the man on the ship and the strange crate. But no one knew anything and no one else had seen the shadowy form. They said the lad was mazed.*

---

*   Mazed: fooled, mistaken, led astray.

'Some years afterwards, the youth had grown into a young man and had become an exciseman. Another vessel was brought into port, under identical circumstances, and he, with another officer, was placed in charge of her. They took turns to stand watch. One evening he sat alone in the state cabin. Opposite him was a large empty armchair. But as he watched, there appeared in it the figure of a gentleman, richly clothed, holding in his hand a music box, and on his knee sat a little boy, who was playing with him, and clasping his neck.

'As he stared on this ghostly scene, the young exciseman's hair stiffened, he was transfixed with pain between his shoulder blades and all his senses were strung to a pitch of unearthly tension. He was incapable of speech or movement.

'Eventually the other exciseman came to relieve him. He found the young officer paralysed in a state of terror. Opposite him the chair was empty, but no one had been seen leaving the ship and no one ever saw the gentleman or the little boy again.'

'What happened to the exciseman after that?' asked Jamie.

'In time he got over it, but he would tell his tale to anyone who would listen. I've heard it lots of times; he's my dad.'

THE GIRL IN THE BLUE CLOAK

Mr Maybee smiled.

'I can tell you a ghost story; it's well-known here.

'It's about Ann Batten, a St Mary's girl, born in 1745. She worked up at the Garrison back in the time when Captain Bufton was the commandant. She was a pretty lass, always seen in a long dress and a blue cloak. But when she was 19, one night some evil fellow forced himself on her up on the Heugh and left her expecting a baby. I don't know if he was a soldier, a sailor, or a candlestick-maker, but he went on his way and left her in the lurch.

'Well, I don't know if she was disowned, or if she somehow kept her situation secret. Either way is pretty sad. She gave birth to her baby alone in a small, dark, room in the servants' quarters at Star Castle. She must have been terrified, in pain, maybe injured.

'Some people say the baby was stillborn. Others say he was sickly and could never have survived. Others say that she accidentally dropped him onto the stone flags. But after seven days the poor little chap was found dead in a box wrapped in brown paper and tied up with string.

'Ann was tried for manslaughter at Star Castle on 10 September 1765. But the twelve men of Scilly couldn't reach a verdict so she was sent to Cornwall for a retrial. There she was acquitted. Now that might have been the end of a rather sad story. Poor Ann would have been quickly forgotten.

'But after the trial no one knew what became of her. Some say that one stormy night Ann threw herself off the Garrison headland and was drowned. But not long after, watchers on the Garrison saw a young woman in a long dress and a blue cloak hurrying through the dusk. Again and again people have seen this figure on Garrison Hill, in Star Castle, in Garrison House. It's as if Ann is determined that her tale will be retold and listeners will learn from it.

If you keep your eyes open after sunset you may see her, too.

AT WAR WITH THE NETHERLANDS

'We must be on our way,' said Anthony. 'Thank you for your hospitality.' Then he added thoughtfully, 'I don't think we'll revisit Hugh Town just yet though.'

'Quite right,' said William Maybee. 'There may be Dutchmen there!'

'All the Dutchmen I've met were kindly people.'

'Maybe,' said Maybee, 'but you have to watch for them here! During the Civil War the Dutch sent Admiral Tromp to get reparation for the losses caused by Royalist privateers. As he got no good response, he declared war on the Isles of Scilly. But then Cromwell's man, Admiral Blake, made the Royalists surrender. The Dutchmen went home without firing a shot. But they forgot to declare peace, so in theory the Dutch are still at war with the Isles of Scilly. It's the longest war ever known and the only one in which neither side has actually fired at each other.'*

---

*   The Dutch ambassador visited the isles to sign a treaty and peace was declared on
     17 April 1986, 335 years after the 'war' began.

THE GIANTS OF ST MARY'S

So, Anthony and Jamie left Peninnis. They followed a path that led north and east. They heard a cry.

'Hey wait for me!' It was Lizzie. 'You need someone to show you the way, don't you? Please don't send me back. My dad knows I'm with you; he said it would be all right.'

Anthony smiled at Lizzie's enthusiasm.

'What do you reckon, Jamie?'

'Ooh, I don't know.'

'Oh please!'

'Come on,' said Anthony. 'Before the weather changes.'

The path headed north. Ahead of them was Buzza Hill.

'You know about the giants?' asked Lizzie. 'Once there were lots on the Isles of Scilly, and some are still here.

'On St Agnes they would gather to celebrate, for there they had a giant's Punch Bowl, but St Mary's was their favourite place.

'In the east of St Mary's they had a Giant's Chair, where they would sit and watch the sun rise over the cliffs of Cornwall.

'In the south they had the Giants' Castle, where they would watch for ships from warmer climes, bringing oranges and grapes and sweet dark wine.

'But in the west of St Mary's they would watch the sun go down over the islands and set in golden fire beyond the great wastes of the ocean, and there they would take their rest. Indeed, there is still a giant sleeping on Carn Mahael on the west side of Peninnis.

'Ahead of us is Buzza's Hill. On the summit lived a giant called Buzza. He founded the Buzza family who live in Cornwall to this very day, though now they have shrunk to a more reasonable size! Old Buzza was a great storyteller and in the evening he would tell stories to the other giants as the stars appeared in the sky.

'On Buzza Hill are the graves of those ancient people. The islanders won't touch them: they say that Buzza and his friends aren't dead at all, they are just sleeping, and who knows what happens when you wake up a giant?

'In 1756 a man called William Borlase wanted to open the graves to see what was inside. But as he began, the clouds gathered. The thunder rolled and the lighting flashed. The wind bowed the trees and tore the thatch from the roofs. The excavation was halted straight away. The islanders told Borlase that the storm was brought on them by the wrath of the giants whose sleep was being disturbed.

'So if you go up Buzza Hill, tread lightly; you never know who you might awaken.'

THE LEGEND OF TOLMAN HEAD

In the afternoon sun the travellers continued towards Old Town Bay, where Jamie had landed days before. The bay was shallow with the remains of an old quay at its head. On the beach men and women gathered seaweed.

Old Town itself was just a handful of cottages. Behind them were the remains of Ennor Castle.

Said Anthony, 'In 1540, the King's Antiquary, John Leland, called the castle "a meately strong pile". In 1554 it still had cannon; but after that it was abandoned.'

'This used to be the main port,' said Lizzie, 'but when the wind is from the south-east it's not a good harbour. These days most ships go into St Mary's Pool. That headland over on the other side is called Tolman Head.'

Soon they reached the church, sadly in need of repair. The sexton was at the churchyard gate and he gave them a wave.

'Storytellers, eh? I can tell you a tale about this place.'

Richard, Earl of Cornwall, was richer than many kings because of the taxes he got from Cornish tin mines. It was he that endowed Tresco monastery.

He gave the monks the right to the profit from all wrecks, which denied the poor islanders that part of their income. But to cap it all, one prior imposed a tax on everyone landing on St Mary's, just for the privilege of stepping ashore.

The toll even applied to local fishermen and to pilgrims who elsewhere were always allowed free passage. Eventually the locals complained to their earl.

One May evening a ship arrived in Old Town Cove. Pilgrims came ashore, led by one taller than the rest. He wore a cloak, and a deep-brimmed hat hid his face.

At the Toll House a chain and padlock barred the way. That day the toll monk had been sent on an errand so the Prior himself controlled access. He was studying some liturgy and told the pilgrims to wait. But their leader was in no mood to delay. 'Come now,' he said sternly, 'Let us pass. There is no toll for such as we.'

The old Prior was both deaf and unsympathetic to such complaints. He glanced up but said nothing. But then the leader of the pilgrims vaulted over the chain to where the Prior was sitting, clearly very angry. But the proud Prior was used to obedience. He stood erect, placed his hand on the pilgrim's chest and told him to him stand back.

But then the pilgrim cast aside his cloak, raised a mailed fist, and struck the old man on the head. As the Prior sank to the ground, he looked up to see it was none other than Richard, Earl of Cornwall.

The shock and the blow were too much for the old Prior. As he breathed his last he whispered, 'Lord Earl, that blow has stricken both thy house and thee'. Then he spoke no more.

Earl Richard was full of remorse. He abolished the toll but he recompensed the monks for their loss of income and he founded a chantry where masses were said every day for the soul of the Prior.

But from that moment the Earl's luck left him. His riches wasted away and he went to the grave a broken man.

Old Town was never the same. There were constant storms, so sailors shunned it. The church was damaged. It was haunted by the ghost of the dead prior, who was often seen on the headland asking for tolls from other spectral figures.

The castle fell into disrepair and was abandoned. People took the stone to build new houses or repair old ones. The sea and sand advanced on Old Town until only a few cottages remained. It is still a sad place, waiting to be lost beneath earth or water. Soon all that will remain will be this story.

With that the sexton retreated into his church.

'Goodness,' said Jamie, 'do you think that's true?'

Lizzie chimed in, 'In those days ships were small and there weren't many of them. But as ships became larger, they preferred to anchor in St Mary's Pool. Hugh Town grew and Star Castle was built. That's why Old Town declined and Ennor Castle was abandoned.'

Anthony agreed. 'I don't believe a word of it! The monks on Tresco did charge for using St Helen's Pool, but there is no record of a levy for Old Town Cove. But think about the name: Tolman Head. I think this is a new story invented to explain the name of the headland. But 'Tolman' doesn't mean 'a man who charged tolls'. Tolman comes from two Cornish words: 'maen', which means stone, and 'tol' meaning hole. If we explore the headland, I'm sure we'll find a stone with a hole in it. The hole in the stone is the hole in the story!'

Then a familiar figure appeared in the lane. Jamie called out, 'Aunt Polly!'

'Jamie!' she smiled. 'Now Lizzie I know and you sir must be Jamie's dad. Mary Jenkin is my name. If you can spare the time, Old Town would love to hear your news, and some drollery would not go amiss!'

TOM BUTT'S BED

Next day they headed east across Salakee Down. Soon they reached the impressive cliffs of the Giant's Castle.

'My dad says it's a very old fort,' said Lizzie, 'and just down there is a secret cave. You can't see it from above. It's called Tom Butt's bed.'

In the time of Queen Anne there was a lad called Tom Butt. Tom was a poor servant boy; he worked at Salakee Farm. But there he was treated cruelly by his master. He would beat Tom given the slightest excuse or none at all. Tom's only free time was to go to church in Old Town on Sundays and saint's days. Tom longed to leave his cruel master, escape the islands and see the world.

One day as he was watching the sea birds, out at sea he saw a naval ship on the horizon. Such visits were common – ships would often wait in the sheltered waters of St Mary's Pool for the tide to take them up-channel, take on fresh water or pick up a pilot to guide them into Falmouth or Plymouth.

But this ship was different. After it anchored, three cutters rowed swiftly ashore. Then the press gang started combing the public houses and byways for fit young men to force into the Navy.

But the small community could not afford to lose any men – they were vital as boatmen and as farm labourers. The cruel reputation of the press gang was well known. So sailors and farmers alike hid their young men in sail lofts and barns so they would not be captured. All but Tom's master, who cared nothing for his young servant and did nothing to protect him.

Tom fled the farm in fear, desperately looking for somewhere to hide. The downs gave no cover at all, but below the steep cliffs east of the Giant's Castle he found a cave, invisible from above, so there he hid.

But it so happened that three boys were out hunting rabbits with their dogs. The dogs picked up an unusual scent and rushed, howling and barking to the cave.

'Shhh!' whispered Tom, before the boys could call out and attract more attention. 'I'm hiding from the press gang.' They agreed they would secretly bring him what food they could.

The press gang searched here and there. Tom's master searched high and low. But Tom stayed in his cave, safely hidden. Before dawn and after dusk his three young friends brought him what food they could.

After three days and three nights, from the mouth of the cave Tom saw the ship sailing away to the east. Tom's master gave up searching, thinking that Tom must have been pressed.

That night Tom slipped into town, stowed away on a trading schooner and sailed off to see the world, just as he had always dreamed. But he is remembered to this day, for the cave is known as Tom Butt's Bed.

SONGS AND SHIPWRECKS

Then the path turned north to Porth Hellick. As they walked, Lizzie sang:

Farewell and adieu to you fair Spanish Ladies,
Farewell and adieu to you ladies of Spain
For we've received orders to sail for old England
But we hope in a short time to see you again.

Everyone joined in the chorus:

> We'll rant and we'll roar like true British sailors,
> We'll rant and we'll roar across the salt seas,
> Until we strike soundings in the Channel of old England,
> From Ushant to Scilly 'tis thirty-five leagues.

Lizzie continued:

> We hove our ship to, with the wind at sou'west, my boys,
> We hove our ship to, for to strike soundings clear;
> We had 45 fathoms with a white sandy bottom,
> So we squared our main yard and up-Channel did steer.

> The first land we sighted was calléd the Dead man,
> Next Ram's Head off Plymouth, Start, Portland and Wight;
> We sailed in by Beachy, by Fairley and Dungeness
> And then we bore up for the South Foreland light

> Then the signal was made for the grand fleet to anchor
> And all in the Downs that night for to lie;
> Let go your shank painter, let go your cat stopper,
> Haul up your clew-garnets, let tacks and sheets fly!

> Now let ev'ry man drink off his full bumper
> And let ev'ry man drink off his full glass;
> We'll drink and be jolly and drown melancholy
> And here's to the health of each true-hearted lass.

Everyone sang choruses between the verses.

'It's a naval song,' said Anthony. 'It describes the Grand Fleet on a voyage from Spain to the Downs.'

'Aren't "downs" hills?' asked Jamie.

'These downs are an anchorage between Ramsgate and Dover. Ships wait there for the wind and tide to take them into the Thames or the North Sea or the English Channel.

'After crossing Biscay, before turning up-channel, ships would check their position by a running fix on Ushant or by soundings. In the song the depth tells us they were at the start of the Channel and the sandy bottom tells us they are north of the rock ledges off Ushant. The "dead man" is Dodman, east of Falmouth. Ram's Head is Rame Head by Torpoint.

'But you can tell the song was written before Trinity House surveyed the coast. From Ushant to Scilly isn't 35 leagues, it's 32 leagues. On the old charts the Isles of Scilly were plotted about 10 miles north of their true position. I wonder how many ships were lost because of that?

'The only other song I know about Scilly is "The Scilly Wreck", which has a press-ganged sailor, a shipwreck, great loss of life and grieving sweethearts. It reflects very well the danger of inaccurate charts.'

THE WRECK OF THE *ASSOCIATION*

At the head of Porth Hellick was a memorial. Nearby in the sands was a shallow pit.

'Even in storms it never fills with sand. Nothing ever grows in it,' said Lizzie.

'You have a choice,' she said. 'I can tell you what I think is true or I can tell you tales about what might have happened.'

'I think we'd better have both,' said Anthony, 'then we can put fact alongside fiction and see what we get.'

Lizzie began.

'Sir Cloudesley Shovell was a famous admiral and the *Association* was his flagship. In 1707 his fleet was sailing home from Gibraltar – twenty-one ships. They reached the mouth of the English Channel on the night of 22 October.

'The weather was bad and navigation almost impossible. The Admiral ordered the fleet to heave to and then he held a conference of captains. All but one thought they were off Ushant, so they sailed on. But the ships were actually much further north and as night fell they sailed into the Western Rocks. The *Association* struck the Outer Gilstone and sank in three or four minutes. All her crew were lost,

including the admiral. The *Firebrand*, *Rodney* and *Eagle* were also lost. Some 2,000 men drowned. It was the greatest disaster in British maritime history.

'From the three biggest ships just one crewman survived. Clinging to a spar, he was carried to the Hellwethers, west of St Agnes.

'Next day, floating on a hatch, the body of Sir Cloudesley washed ashore in Porth Hellick; his pet dog was not far away. He was found by a soldier from St Mary's Garrison and his wife. They buried him in the sand, after taking a diamond ring from his finger to help identification.

'The ring was sent to Lady Shovell, who confirmed it was Sir Cloudesley's. She was grateful to the soldier for giving her husband a decent burial, so she gave him a pension for life.

'Sir Cloudesley's body was exhumed and embalmed. Then it was carried to Plymouth, lying in state in the Citadel, until Lady Shovell had it taken to her home in Soho Square, London. On 22 December Sir Cloudesley was carried in state to Westminster Abbey and buried among heroes of renown, with the sad story written on his tombstone.

'This shallow pit is where the soldier and his wife first buried Cloudesley Shovell. Scillonians say that because Cloudesley refused to heed a warning and wantonly threw away so many lives, God keeps alive the memory of his wickedness by letting no grass grow here.'

'A sorry tale indeed,' said Anthony. 'But, you mentioned a warning. I think you have more to tell us.'

THE QUARTERMASTER'S TALE

Lizzie continued: 'Have you heard of reading the waves? It's a skill some seamen have; they know the sea so well that they can tell where they are from the way the waves break.

'Remember the sailor that was washed onto the Hellwethers? John Troutbeck, Chaplain of the Isles, wrote that he was the only survivor from the *Association*. He was the quartermaster and, when he had recovered from his ordeal, he explained that on the *Association* there was a Scillonian who could read the waves. This man had told his shipmates that unless they changed course they would soon be among the rocks of Scilly.

'When the ship's officers heard this, he was ordered to be punished for trying to raise a mutiny. Troutbeck says that when the ship struck, only that man survived.'

'That doesn't sound right.'

'I agree, it's a tale told by the sole survivor that says that someone else is the sole survivor! And in truth the quartermaster who supposedly told the tale was from HMS *Romney*, not the *Association* – George Lawrence, his name was, a butcher by trade. Also, as quartermaster he would have been a Petty Officer not an ordinary sailor, so he wasn't talking about himself.'

THE PUBLICAN'S TALE

'What do other people say?'

'In Hugh Town they say that the admiral was so vexed that a common sailor should claim to know better than his officers that he ordered him to be hanged for insubordination.

'The sailor begged that the chaplain should read him one of the Psalms before his execution. His request was granted and he chose

the 109th Psalm, repeating in a loud voice all
the curses it contains.* With his last breath he
prophesied that those who caused his death
would find a watery grave.

'Till then the weather had been fine, but as
soon as his body was committed to the sea a
gale began. Then his shipmates were horrified
to see the corpse out of its winding sheet, face
up, following in their wake. They knew they
were doomed.'

'It's a good tale,' said Anthony, 'but if no one
survived to tell the tale, how do we know what the tale was?'

'It's a mystery,' said Lizzie. 'And here's another.'

THE PAYMASTER AND THE PARSON

'Lady Shovell offered a large reward for the recovery of any of the
admiral's property. In 1709 Edmund Herbert, later Paymaster of the
Royal Marines, came searching. He didn't find any valuables, but he
did find that the wreck was still talked about. He heard it said that
before the soldier from the Garrison found Sir Cloudesley's body, two
local women had "strip't off his shirt" and had "taken a ring, which
however left ye impression on his finger".

'As the soldier also took a ring, then the admiral must have been
wearing at least two rings. The soldier and his lady are unlikely to
have reached Porth Hellick from the Garrison before 9 a.m. The local
women, possibly employed on domestic or farm duties at Salakee or
Carn Friars, could have found the body hours earlier.

'Some twenty-eight years later the rest of the tale emerged.
Sir Cloudesley's grandson himself used to tell this.

'On her death bed one of those women summoned the parson to
make a confession. She told him that the admiral was just alive when
found, so she smothered him and took various possessions including

---

*   Psalm 109: A Prayer for the Punishment of the Wicked, aka 'The Cursing Psalm'.

the priceless emerald ring given him by his lifelong friend James, 3rd Earl of Berkeley. But she had been afraid to sell the ring and as the confession ended she gave it to the minister. He, in turn, apparently returned it to James Berkeley. But now, though the Berkeley family have the story, they haven't got the ring and no one knows where it is! No one knows if the tale is true or false.'

'But the confessional is secret,' said Anthony. 'How do we know the tale at all?'

THE GIANT'S HOUSE

They left the bay with its sad memorial and headed up onto Porth Hellick Down. To the left, over the fields, they could see Carn Friars farm. But in less than five minutes they reached an amazing structure – a huge circular mound about 13 yards in diameter. Jamie had seen nothing like it before.

'It's a giant's house,' said Lizzie, 'let's go inside.'

They ran down a passage running from the edge of the mound towards the centre and then ducked into a rectangular chamber, about 4 yards long and 5ft high.

'This is great,' said Lizzie. 'We could shelter here.'

'But what if the giant comes back?' asked Jamie.

'I bet I could find somewhere more comfortable,' came Anthony's cheery voice from the outside.

'This will be thousands of years old,' said Anthony, 'but I don't think it's a giants' house, I think it's what some call a Druids' Grave. Mr Borlase wrote about such things.

'When it was built the sea would have been much lower and it would have been high above the sea. It must have been very imposing – the grave of a great king or warrior.'

Then Lizzie suggested, 'Let's go to Holy Vale. The farmer is friendly and I'm sure they'd like to hear a story.'

So they walked inland to Holy Vale, where the farmer let them stay in an outlying barn. 'Come to the house for supper at sunset,' he said, 'and I'll tell you a tale about this place.'

A LEGEND OF HOLY VALE

Holy Vale, known as Le Val in Norman times, lies between Maypole and Porth Hellick. Its small fields suggest cultivation from early times. Polwhele wrote: 'The monks of Trescaw … cleared Holy Vale of its woods and modelled in into what it is.' Borlase added that it 'received every kind of improvement from its monastical proprietors'. The claims may be true, for we know that the monks of Tresco owned three 'fields' on St Mary's.

Henry Whitfield wrote that Holy Vale has 'remembered sanctity'. He imagined a convent there and a miraculous rose bush dedicated to the Virgin. This is his tale.

It was the Tuesday after Easter. Holy Vale was beautiful with blossom and greenery. The day was bright and local people strove to make it yet brighter. After the restraint of Lent, it was now time for fun: it was the day of 'misrule'. Choirboys, farm workers and all-comers dressed as the abbot and monks of misrule, a dragon, and the great tempter himself. Little children dressed as angels.

But something else was happening: a solemn ceremony in the convent chapel. The profession of a sister is always important, but the young woman then to be dedicated to God had an unusual story. ...

She was brought up in seclusion in Ennor Castle by the aged Dame de Barentin. It was said she was an orphan. No one knew who her parents were, nor her name. She was just called the Demoiselle Maude and was treated with great respect, almost as royalty.

She was beautiful and intelligent. Her teachers could do no more. The brother limner from Tresco was surpassed by her exquisite work.* The Bible, illuminated by her, was worth a king's ransom. The convent's broideress was amazed. Yet Maude had the innocence of a child. There was just one clue to her identity: her face. Though gentle and loving, she had a look that brooked neither familiarity nor intrusion. Some saw but never mentioned a spark of Plantagenet in her eye.

It seemed that Maud was to be kept in the castle until of marriageable age. Her days were peaceful if monotonous. The castle had few visitors and they were seldom young. Pilgrims and priests brought news, but they talked to Dame de Barentin and Maude was left to her own thoughts.

However, in the castle there was another young person: Jocelyn de St Martin, the Dame's page, whose ambition was to become a squire to the Earl of Cornwall. He was the same age as Maude and they had known each other from childhood. No word had been whispered, no pledge made, no token exchanged. But that youth loved the maiden and she smiled to know that she was loved. But one day as they gazed into each other's eyes they were seen by the Dame de Barentin.

Straight away Jocelyn was sent with a letter for the Earl. Instantly he was made the Earl's squire, obliged to remain with him in Launceston Castle.

The Earl decreed that Maude should marry no one of birth inferior to her own. A commission annulling the usual period of probation was sent by John Grandison, Bishop of Exeter, to Robert Deneys, Lord Prior of Scilly. The Dame de Barentin took the unsuspecting Maude to Holy Vale. There she was taken to a cell, where the Abbess told her she was immediately to become a novice nun.

---

* A limner is an illuminator of manuscripts.

Maude did not argue or complain, for Plantagenet spirit was in her heart. Serenely she laid aside her finery. She unloosed the silken volumes of her dark hair, which the Abbess severed, lock by lock. When the rites were concluded, she came forward and received the kisses of the Abbess and the nuns with a cheek so cold that it froze the lips that touched it. Then she returned to her cell, her living tomb, serene as before.

Her tirewoman* had, as a favour, been left with her. As soon as they were alone, she fell at the feet of her lady, now called Sister Mary, full of indignation and compassion. But the high-born damsel raised her up and silently kissed her brow. Her eye was glassy, her smile was stiff; they spoke of something fearful within. But whatever she felt, she said nothing. The tirewoman, who loved her mistress, was amazed, but Sister Mary gently sent her on her way.

That evening at vespers Mary asked if she might be allowed to remain that night in prayer before the altar. It was not unusual for a novice to pray to the Virgin for support and comfort, so the request was granted. From then it seemed that a shadow was cast across her. The girl had gone; a nun remained. She seldom spoke and never complained. Her tirewoman visited often, staying for hours in her cell. Mary did not mix with the other sisters. Her main task was the care of a miraculous rose bush, consecrated to the Virgin. It was due to this bush that the place was called Holy Vale. Its flowers were said to have the power to preserve the wearer from mortal sin. The bush had the gift of perpetual spring and blossomed all year long. She always wore one of its buds on her bosom.

---

* 	A tirewoman is a wardrobe mistress.

So passed her novitiate. Winter melted into spring. Easter was past and the day approached when the irrevocable black veil was to be donned. But Mary remained as cold, as formal as ever. Her faithful tirewoman spent with her the eve of the fatal day.

After vespers Sister Mary again asked to spend the night in the chapel to prepare for the next day's ceremony. The Abbess said yes, then Mary went alone to the high altar and there was glimpsed like a prostrate statue, absorbed in prayer.

But next day, when the Abbess and sisters went to the chapel Mary was not there. Her cell was empty. She had vanished. There was just one clue: at the rosebush of the Virgin, a bough was broken off and lay on the ground, and one bud was taken from its stem. They looked high and low, but of Mary there was no sign.

When the Earl was told, his wrath was terrible. The sisters lamented and prayed. But all was in vain. Sister Mary was missed for a while, but as the months passed she faded from memory. Her name was hardly mentioned; her place was filled by another; her memory was just a tale.

Years passed lightly over the community of Holy Vale. One by one the sisters were called from their earthly duties to higher things. The Abbess bequeathed her sceptre to another. Only two sisters remained who had known Sister Mary.

Then came a year when Easter was late and Holy Vale was beautiful with blossom and greenery. In profusion the rose bush bore its earliest and choicest blooms.

Once again it was the time of misrule and celebration.

On the eve of Easter Tuesday there was a solemn mass for sister Mary. But as it was sung, a spirit of peace, a sacred blessing, seemed to descend on the chapel. An angelic voice seemed to mingle with the choir.

Next morning the doors of the chapel were opened for matins. But the Abbess, at the head of her train, found she was not the first to enter.

A figure lay before the altar, its hands clasped in prayer, as still as a marble effigy on a tomb. In her lifeless face was peace and on her lips were a smile.

It was a young woman, dressed as a novice nun. Over her heart was a rosebud, apparently long gathered, but somehow as fresh as if newly plucked. The sisters crowded round. The two oldest knew at once it was sister Mary. No one knew by what miracle she had been preserved and returned. She seemed as young and innocent as the day she vanished.

But for the two older sisters there was no one to ask after her fate. The Earl was dead. Jocelyn de St Martin had died in the crusades. Some spoke of a secret passage from the chapel, by which she had fled to join her faithful tirewoman, but nothing was ever found.

They buried her where she lay, beautiful and holy, the rosebud in her hand. Such was her aura of sanctity that a chapel dedicated to holy Maude was built in Hugh Town.

At the Reformation, the black marble slab above her grave was destroyed, but, according to tradition, it read, 'Cy git Marie, priez pour elle. *Here lies Mary, pray for her.*'

If it ever existed, the convent described by Whitfield is long gone. But in Holy Vale there still grows a rose bush; it blossoms the whole year round.

'I know where the chapel was in Hugh Town,' said Lizzie. 'It's near the Quay. Some still call it Maudut's Chapel. It's a house with a steep roof. They found bones in the garden.'

Anthony spoke: 'I don't think there was ever a convent here. But it's a clever story; I wonder where it came from?'

THE SHOTGUN AND THE SERVING MAID

That night in the barn they slept well. Next morning was unusually still. Dust motes floated in the first shafts of light. Shadows caressed the old stone walls. The three travellers were in the blissful borderland between sleeping and waking. Suddenly all were launched into a fearful wakefulness by the sound of a gunshot followed by an agonised scream.

Jamie and Lizzie ran outside. There was not a soul in sight. They all hurried to the farmhouse, where the clock was striking eight.

'What was that?' cried Lizzie.

The farmer looked puzzled.

'The gunshot, the scream, surely you heard.'

The farmer looked embarrassed. 'I should have told you. Sit down, have some breakfast and I'll tell you the story.'

'About seventy-five years ago, not far from here, was the farm of a man called James Uren. James had a daughter Elizabeth, just 13 she was. Sadly his wife died shortly after Elizabeth was born, so James employed a servant girl called Bess, who worked about the house and farm.

'It was nearly eight o'clock on the thirteenth of May 1730. Young Elizabeth was making breakfast for the family. Bess was in the yard doing the washing. Farmer James was some distance away in the barn looking out towards Crow Sound, the very same barn you were sleeping in.

'Suddenly the quiet of the morning was shattered. James Uren heard a gunshot followed by an agonised scream. He sprinted from the barn to investigate. The only firearm on the farm was his shotgun, which was kept on the wall in the farmhouse, and no one else was allowed to touch it. At the house he found his daughter on the ground, bleeding profusely from a gunshot wound in her groin. He rushed to her side and held her in his arms. She smiled weakly, saying that Bess had shot her. Then her eyes closed. James tried to stem the flow of blood, but soon his daughter was dead.

'James Uren shouted for Bess. She had been alone with Elizabeth in the house; there was no one else to blame. Angrily he demanded an explanation. Bess explained that 'the little girl was then giving her such saucy language as she did not like to hear'. To frighten her and make her stop, Bess took down the gun, thinking it was unloaded. James Uren swore an oath. Normally he unloaded his gun after use, but the last time he must have forgotten to do so.

'Next day, after an inquest, Elizabeth was buried in Old Town churchyard.

'Bess was sent for trial at Cornwall County Assizes. There she was acquitted. It was determined that the shooting was a tragic accident after a foolish argument had gone too far.

'The Uren farmhouse burned to the ground on Christmas Day in 1763, but the barn remains, and that's where you spent last night.

But it's as if the old stones have a memory of what happened and sometimes, when they choose, they pass it on.'

'Sad,' said Anthony. 'Take it from me, as an old soldier, you should never play with guns. Never, ever point them at someone in jest; you just never know.'

As they continued on their way, Lizzie gave a running commentary.

At Maypole she announced, 'On May Day we come here to dance the summer in. They give us children bread and cream. And on 5 November we have a bonfire here.'

At Pelistry Anthony added, 'Pol Lystry, pool for small boats.'

'That's right,' said Lizzie. 'If there's a southerly wind and fishermen can't get into Old Town Cove they come here.'

In the cove was a small island with fortifications.

'Pellew's Redoubt, in case Napoleon comes.'

Along the coast there were more batteries, ramparts and block houses. At Innisidgen they explored the carns with their prehistoric graves, then continued west to Sandy Bar.

There Lizzie announced, 'This is where the causeway went to St Martin's and Tresco. Now the water's far too deep but ships sometimes run aground here at low tide.'

RIVALS

The families of Webber and Woodcock once lived above Sandy Bar. No one knew where they came from; some said it was from a privateer wrecked there many years ago.

Legend has that the Banfields and Mumfords came to Scilly together. Sailing through Crow Sound, they saw the huts above Sandy Bar. A glance from one of them annoyed a Webber or a Woodcock and so began their feud.

In time, Banfields and Mumfords became members of the Council of Twelve presiding over the islands in Hugh Town. The Webbers and Woodcocks stayed on the other side of the island.

But in 1742 one of the Council, Sidney Banfield, called a Webber a 'wrecker'. Whilst technically correct, this was also true of the whole population; all relied on flotsam, jetsam and wreck for their liveli-hood. But the Woodcocks and Webbers were different. They lived on the other side of the island.

Blind to any hypocrisy, the Council, acting as prosecution, judge and jury, condemned the Webbers and Woodcocks and ruled that they should be made to live in Hugh Town, under the watchful eye of the Garrison.

Next day, old Liqueur Webber sat on a rock loading his musket. Behind him were the dunes above Sandy Bar and the homes of his family. He had already heard of the Council's plan and he had no intention of moving. Then a messenger brought news that a boat had left Hugh Town heading north. Soon it was in sight. In it Liqueur recognised Ensign Charles of the Garrison and Constable Bogun.

'Darn it!' said Bogun. 'It's a trap for sure. How did Webber know we were coming? What's to do: step ashore and face a musket ball, or return and be prisoned for not obeying orders?'

'Step ashore,' mocked Liqueur, and he lowered his gun.

The ensign and the constable picked their way up the pebble slope to where Old Liqueur sat, his gun on his knees. Then he called them to halt, 'Is your errand of peace or war, of threat or knavery? Do your masters dare not come themselves? What does their greed demand this time?'

Constable Bogun pulled out the message and began to read, though in truth it was no reading for he had learned it by rote and his eyes were fixed on Webber's musket:

Whereas Liqueur Webber and his families and Dice-box Woodcock and his families have made themselves objectionable, dangerous to the safety of the inhabitants of the island of St Mary's, and of ill repute on the coast, it is thought necessary by Charles Jeffreyson, Esquire, Commandant and Chief Magistrate of all His Majesty's Garrisons and Islands of Scilly, and by and with the advice of the Council of the said islands, to remove them from their present position. It has been directed by the authorities aforesaid that the younger families, six of Webber's and five of Woodcock's, shall repair to Mary's Walls of Mount Todden battery, there living and taking their part in the defence of said battery; while the youngest of these families shall attend a school, and the grandparents shall dwell under the walls of Mount Hollis battery of the Hugh, ready for service if necessary when the warning gun shall fire from the Garrison. For provision and maintenance land shall be allotted to such families to work upon; so justice shall be fulfilled and these Islands of Scilly benefited and held in better defence and repute for His Majesty King George. The safety ...

'Git back to the boat,' shouted Liqueur, lifting his gun.

'We are going,' said Constable Bogun, 'but there's ...'

'Go!' thundered Liqueur and then appeared eight armed relatives who had been in hiding.

Bogun and Charles beat a hasty retreat, though the ensign paused halfway down the beach and shouted back, 'If not complied with within three days, the military will be sent to enforce it.'

'And,' called Bogun, 'you will be imprisoned for disobeying the Commandant and the Council of Twel ...'

The sentence ended abruptly as a musket ball from Liqueur hastened his visitors on their way.

Then the Webbers and Woodcocks held a council of war. It took place outdoors, both for secrecy's sake and as a precaution against being trapped together.

Sheep and cattle grazed nearby; above them the sun was shining; the blue sea lapped the shore. From a distance it could have looked like a picnic party.

'Fight them,' said Dice-box Woodcock. 'Defy Jeffreyson and the Council of Twelve! Who ever knew them act without self-interest? Who raced us to the shore when the last wreck came in? It was them!'

One of Dice-box's sons spoke. 'Why should they order us about? We mind our own business. But when we get anything they want it. Now we are ordered from our houses and our families separated for the greater peace of St Mary's. The peace! Who breaks the peace but them? They call us wreckers, but others go scathless. They call us the black spot amid the fair islands, yet they want us for defence. While we defended the walls others would be robbing us.'

A young Webber, wildly excited, thrust himself forward.

'We are twenty families, equal to the Commandant's men, for all our women can take their stand by the guns.'

'And,' said a more cautious voice, 'be caught and jailed, maybe shipped to a London prison. I am for liberty, but I would not seek violence.'

Liqueur's eldest son, Slash-cut, now stood. His nickname came from a blue scar on his face, the result, some said, of a wound got when raiding a wrecked but not abandoned vessel. He spoke in grunts punctuated with loud hisses of breath.

'We're in for bloodshed,' he said. 'And just as well. I want to finish with 'em. We will not go into the Hugh to live amongst people who are not of us. There is nothing to be done but draw red blood, military blood, Council blood.'

Old Liqueur waved his musket. 'I'm not so sure,' he said. 'We don't need the rattle of muskets and swords unless the Council insist. There is another way.'

'Cut down those at the bottom of this?' enquired a young Woodcock. 'Have it out with the Banfields and Mumfords?'

'The only way,' said Slash-cut, 'is to fight for our homes.'

'Whatever happens we shall lose them,' said Liqueur. 'If we fight and win, the Commandant will send for help; the Council will ask Lord Godolphin for aid. There will be more fighting with no good result. We do not want slaughter, but we do want our unity and independence. I have a plan.'

Then old Liqueur revealed his ideas. He was greeted first with doubt, then with interest, and finally with applause.

The three days' notice elapsed. There were no Webbers in Hugh Town. The Commandant and Council gathered their soldiers and constables to march to Sandy Bar.

'We will pull down their houses,' said the Commandant. 'His Lordship's agent has approved it. I have sent men by boat to drive the wreckers towards us, so they cannot escape by water. They will soon be in our hands.'

Confident of success, he left to organise his men.

The march across the island was joined by both citizens and Council, led by curiosity or partiality. Councillors Smith, Gibson, and Edwards had joined Banfield, Mumford and Jeffreyson. All were armed. They had to deal with determined and courageous men and women.

'If they fight,' whispered Gibson to old Edwards, 'the military will not look as grand as now. The Bar people know how to use their weapons.'

'Rouse 'em,' returned Edwards, 'and you know what they can do. They could take the whole island!'

'Better,' concluded Gibson, 'to let 'em keep their distance.'

Jeffreyson spoke to Banfield: 'There will be no trouble. We have the advantage of the hill and with our seaward men we can surround them, perhaps shooting Liqueur as an example. We shall have no difficulty in subduing them.'

Sidney Banfield smiled; he knew that bringing these people into subjection would not be simple.

'My men are in fighting mood,' said Jeffreyson. 'We shall march down the hill and surprise them.'

Above Sandy Bar they moved warily. Ferns and brambles gave them only slight cover, but might conceal their enemies.

The rabble were sent back but they selected their own vantage points; curiosity forbade a return home.

The councillors were allowed to continue; they followed in the rear and with some trepidation.

'I wish it were over,' muttered Mumford. He slipped in a rut and fell flat, standing swiftly to avoid embarrassment.

Councillor Smith sunk to his knees in a hollow, 'As full of pits as Puffin Island and just as treacherous.'

'Hush! There are some of the houses,' quacked old Edwards.

'Got 'em,' whispered Jeffreyson. 'Napping by the look of it. There's not a man in sight. Demmit, is it an ambush?'

The soldiers crept down warily; their allies from the sea landed and all closed in on the hamlet.

'I've got the cramps,' said Gibson, suddenly overcome with an intense desire to hide himself in the heart of a furze bush.

'I shan't go any further,' said Edwards. 'It looks like a trap.'

Then appeared Farmer Downing from Trenoweth, the farm on the hill above the bar.

'What are they looking for?' he asked the councillors.

'Webbers and Woodcocks!' explained Edwards.

'Trouble, murder and satisfaction, and to convince all wreckers that the Commandant, the Council and King George rule,' said Gibson.

By this time the soldiers had reached the dwellings, with no sign of opposition and without a shot being fired.

'Empty, demmit!' shouted Jeffreyson, peering into a deserted hut. It had been stripped of everything movable. The next was empty, too. Every house was empty.

'Gone without my permission. How dare they?'

The Commandant's face was a study in outraged dignity and disappointed revenge.

'They left last night,' said Farmer Downing. 'Just like the Israelites leaving Egypt. There was enough moon to move by, but not enough to reveal them to others. They took their goods, their flocks and herds. Old Liqueur was last to go.'

'Where, where?' asked Mumford.

Downing looked due west. Smoke was rising above the previously uninhabited island of Samson.

'They will build new homes and live without hindrance. If they wish to keep their families together they will. No council will bend them to any purpose but their own. They alone will decide which side of the island they will live on.'

'What will you do?' Banfield asked the Commandant.

'Tell me!' shouted Jeffreyson. 'What can your council do?'

There was no answer. With the sea between, none could intimidate; none could continue a feud.

So, the Webbers and Woodcocks lived untroubled on Samson, right up to the time of Edward Webber the fiery preacher, 'whose piety was equalled by his readiness with the gun, but whose sincerity with both no one doubted.'*

The tale over, the travellers came to Bant's Carn, with its prehistoric village, then strolled south towards Hugh Town.

Soon they were walking along the Strand in the sunshine. On the beach were many small boats being worked on, loaded or unloaded. Then a movement at the quay caught Jamie's eye. Alongside it was Lord Godolphin's ketch. On the deck stood the Penzance Constable and his runner.

*   E.J. Tiddy quotation.

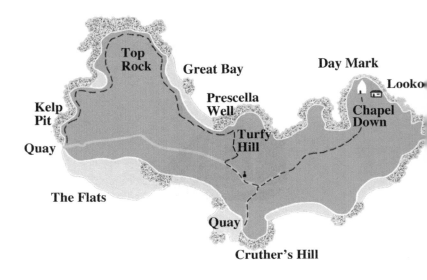

Top
Rock

Great Bay

Day Mark

Looko

Prescella
Well

Chapel
Down

Kelp
Pit

Turfy
Hill

Quay

The Flats

Quay

Cruther's Hill

ST MARTIN'S

0   1/4   1/2

5

PEMP

ST MARTIN'S

St Martin's is a testament to tenacity. Hedges shelter tiny fields from the pervasive wind. Cottages huddle below every horizon, their faces turned hopefully to the sun.

Jamie gently turned Anthony through 180 degrees. Trying to look casual they walked unhurriedly behind the rocky outcrop of Carn Thomas and out of sight of the quay.

'On St Mary's they are sure to catch us,' said Jamie.

'Follow the coast back to Bant's Carn,' said Lizzie. 'Stay in the carn tonight. Just beyond it is an old quay, Pendrathen Quay. I'll meet you there tomorrow morning.'

Next day dawned fine. Jamie was looking for Lizzie across Halangy Down when he heard her voice behind him.

'Come on! We must get across whilst it's still slack water.'

'Across what, and where did you come from?'

'Crow Sound. We're going to see the Ginnicks!'

At the quay was a tiny sailing boat. On the stern was its name, *Kittiwake*. Lizzie confidently raised the sail and soon the little ship was underway.

'Excuse me, Lizzie,' said Anthony. 'What and where are the Ginnicks?'

'They are just north of us! "Ginnicks" are people from St Martin's. Turks are from St Agnes, Thorns from Bryher, Bulldogs from St Mary's and Caterpillars from Tresco.

'We can't get to Agnes, Tresco or Bryher without passing in sight of St Mary's quay. So we're going to St Martin's.'

'That's well thought out,' said Anthony. 'Thank you.'

'The Ginnicks are friendly,' said Lizzie, 'friendly but independent. Around 170 years ago hardly anyone lived here. Now there's a couple of hundred; we'll be safe with them.'

The little boat heeled as it left the lee of the land. Jamie tensed, but Anthony leaned instinctively to windward.

'What are those islands?' asked Jamie, looking east.

'Great Arthur, Little Arthur, Great Ganilly, Little Ganilly, Nornour, there's lots of them. No one lives there now, just the seals and cormorants.'

'Are they named after King Arthur?' asked Jamie.

'I suppose so. But there's a story about Nornour, that little island to the north. They say the goddess Sillina lived there, many, many years ago.'

Soon they were in the lee of St Martin's.

THE FIDDLER OF ST MARTIN'S

'That's Cruther's Point, up there,' said Lizzie, 'and Cruther's Downs beyond it.

'Aha,' said Anthony, 'a famous fiddler!'

Lizzie looked surprised. 'How do you know that?'

'Deduction! Cruther is a Cornish word, sometimes it's written as crowther or crowder. In the Middle Ages a crowther was someone who played the crwth: a fiddle with six strings and a rectangular frame.'

'But how do you know the fiddler was famous?'

'In the thirteenth century people didn't have surnames as we know them; they were often named after their jobs. So I think that a crowther lived here then.

'Being a crowther must have been what distinguished him, or else he would have had a different name. Musical instruments were expensive, often funded by the wealthy, even if played by someone else.

'Other people would have named those places, not the crowther. So he had some local recognition.'

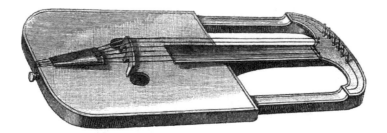

Lizzie smiled, 'So perhaps this crowther was retained to play for the aristocracy and the rest of the time he farmed here on St Martin's. I wonder who he played for?'

'Probably the Blanchminsters or maybe the Godolphins.'

Lizzie turned the craft head to wind and lowered the sail. Two waves later and they were alongside the little quay on Cruther's Point. Lizzie organised mooring lines and Jamie helped Anthony ashore. After a few yards' walk inland they met a dark-suited figure resting on a walking stick.

Lizzie whispered, 'It's Mr Croker from the SPCK. I've seen him at Sunday School – he goes to St Agnes too.'

'Hello, Lizzie,' he said. 'And hello friends of Lizzie. Welcome to the dappled one.'

Greeted with incomprehension, Croker continued, 'St Martin's is named for its saint. But the Celts called this place Brethyoke: the dappled one.'

'Thank you, sir,' replied Anthony, smiling broadly. Cornish fascinated him. As a boy he had been taught to count from one to twenty and recite the Lord's Prayer in Cornish. He learned the language from the old fishermen on the Lizard.

'What brings you here?'

'I, we, are travelling droll-tellers. Storytellers. And you, sir?'

'I am William Croker of the Society for Promoting Christian Knowledge. We have schools on all the islands. Why don't you come to St Martin's church tonight and tell some stories there – it's our one communal building.'

It was agreed and then they continued on to Chapel Down.

DAY MARK AND SIGNAL STATION

'What is that?' Jamie was amazed.

The headland, one of the highest points on the island, was dominated by a huge, stone tower. Beside it was a tall ship's mast supported by six guy ropes. The mast supported a yard from which hung several flag halliards. Nearby was a small enclosure in which stood a tiny cottage with a bunk house, vegetable plot and various outbuildings.

'The stone tower is a day mark,' said Lizzie. 'It's to help ships find their way. That's why it's painted white. The mast is for signalling to ships.'

Jamie described the day mark to Anthony: 'There's a circular tower about 36ft high. On top of that is a tall cone with a small door in it. There's a ledge around the cone and a hand rope so you can walk round the outside.'

On the west side of the day mark was a door. Over the entrance was inscribed 'TE 1683'.

'I expect that's when they started building it,' said Lizzie, 'but I wonder who TE was?'

Inside, a stone staircase curved upwards. Jamie and Lizzie ran up, but at the top they found someone was already there.

'Good morning, young sir, young madam. Trinder, Lieutenant John Trinder, Commander of his Majesty's Signal Station.'

The youngsters gave their names, then they all descended together and Jamie introduced his dad.

The lieutenant called toward the nearby building, 'Mr Mumford! Take over the watch, will you?'

A man emerged and went into the day mark.

'One of my Sea Fencibles,' explained the young lieutenant. 'They share the duties here.'

'It's time for tea,' he announced, and led them to the cottage.

'Put the kettle on Honor, we have guests.'

A pretty young woman appeared.

'Do come in,' she said. 'Enjoy some of our combustibles.'

Anthony suppressed a smile. As the kettle boiled, Honor brought out her special Scillonian Tatty Cake.

'The recipe is a secret,' she said. It was delicious.

'Honor Nance, I was, until 26 November 1808. That was the date of my escapade!'

'Escapade?'

'I escaped from Teän. My father's a kelp burner there. We were the only family on the island. Lonely it was, but my hero came along and now I'm married to the King's Navy.'

'Please,' said Anthony, 'why is the Navy on dry land?'

Lieutenant Trinder answered. 'This is a Naval lookout post and signal station. It's the only one that's made of stone, yet it has the happy quality of being unsinkable! It was built in 1804. As it's so isolated they made this little cottage and bunk room as well.

'We look out for Napoleon's ships, smugglers, pirates and so on. We signal to any ships we don't recognise. If they don't give the correct reply then we know they are unfriendly and we then signal St Mary's. If it's an enemy warship then all naval ships in the area are asked to engage. If it's a smuggler they send out the revenue cutter, the *Providence*.'

'How do you signal?' asked Jamie innocently.

'We use flags, pendants, and ball shapes. A ball above a flag means an enemy frigate or frigates close to the land. Two balls over a flag means a cruiser. Three balls over a flag means a ship of the line.'

'Does it work?' asked Anthony.

'It does indeed,' said Trinder. 'I have a story to prove it.'

FRESH FISH FOR THE FRENCH

Here we often struggle to make ends meet. To help feed their families our men often sell fresh fish to passing ships.

One day a little fishing smack from St Mary's spied a likely-looking ship north of the islands, so they sailed out through Crow Sound to try and sell the crew some of the catch of the day. But when they got close they found that, although the ship was not showing any flags, it was French. It was trying to remain unnoticed! I think it was called *La Virginie*. Before our lads could escape, the Frenchies captured them and sank their little fishing boat.

But here we saw it happen so we hoisted a warning signal. It was seen by Commodore Pellew in the *Indefatigable* and his Western Frigate Squadron found the Frenchman heading towards the Lizard. There was a fierce fight, the French ship was captured and our lads were safely returned home.

'Serves the Frenchies right!' said Lizzie.

'Time for tea,' said Mrs Trinder.

After tea they followed the coast until they reached Bread and Cheese Cove. There they had to eat bread and cheese!

THOMAS EKINS

That evening they joined local people in the tiny church of St Martin. William Croker greeted them.

'Did you reach the day mark?'

'Yes,' said Anthony, 'but Jamie has a question as a result.'

'Please sir,' asked the boy, 'what does T.E. stand for?'

'Aha! You had your eyes open. T.E. stands for Thomas Ekins; a good man he was. He was made Steward of the Islands in about 1660. Thomas was the first steward to live here and work directly with and for the local people. He lived in Hugh Town, in Silver Street,* but from the governor he had a long lease on the island of St Martin's. In those days it was practically deserted, so he persuaded people back to the island, mended slipways and roads, grew hedges to shelter the fields and encouraged people to grow crops.

'He built the day mark and he made this little church too, 1693 it was. He died in 1705 and we have much to thank him for.'

THE STORY OF ST MARTIN

'Do you know about our patron saint?' asked Mr Croker.

---

*   His house is now the Bishop and Wolf Inn.

Lizzie put up her hand. 'I learned it in Sunday School.'

Martin came from Hungary. He was one of the Imperial Cavalry of the Roman Army. But though Christianity was still very new, he became a Christian and was baptised.

One winter's day, Martin was riding along and it started snowing. Beside the road he saw a beggar shivering with the cold. Martin knew that the beggar would die of cold if he was ignored, so Martin took his sword, cut his own cloak in half, and gave half to the beggar.

That night he had a dream. In it he saw Jesus wearing the half cloak that he had given to the beggar and saying to his disciples, 'Here is Martin, the Roman soldier who is now baptised; he has clothed me.'

Martin left the army and became a monk. Such was his piety and wisdom he was made Bishop of Tours in France.

'Well done, Lizzie,' said Mr Croker. 'Yes, Martin died in 397. Such was his holiness that he was made a saint. Old Hallowmas Eve, 11 November, that's St Martin's Day. Sometimes they call it Martinmass.'

Anthony started at the word 'Martinmass'. It brought back childhood memories of hiring fairs, sowing autumn wheat, and 'Martinmas beef'. They seemed an age ago.

THE PREACHERS OF HERESY

'I can tell you a story not many people know,' said Croker. 'Did you see any stones in the ground by the day mark?'

'There were hundreds,' replied Lizzie.

'I know what you mean,' said Jamie. 'North of the day mark there were lines of stones flat in the ground.'

'Well spotted! They are the footings of the walls of a very early chapel. Few people know it is there, but this is its tale.'

At times the early Christian church was turbulent as people argued over how to interpret the scriptures.

In Spain there grew a sect led by Priscillian, the bishop of Avila, west of Madrid. Two of its members were Bishops Instantius and Tiberianus. The sect became an oath-bound society that spread so rapidly it attracted the attention of the Bishops of Aquitaine and Spain.

In about 380, a council of those bishops met at Saragossa and condemned the Priscillians as heretical. One particularly impulsive and violent Spanish bishop, Ithacius of Ossonoba, wrote to the Roman Emperor Gratian, who then deprived Priscillian and his followers of their churches and sentenced them to exile. Priscillian appealed to the Bishop of Milan and the Pope, but without success.

In 383 Gratian was usurped by Magnus Maximus, known to Celts as Macsen Wledig. So Priscillian then appealed to him.

Though opposed to Priscillian, the well-respected Bishop Martin of Tours thought that the intrusion of the Emperor into church matters was wrong. Martin asked the Imperial Court to remove the case from the jurisdiction of the Emperor.

But Bishop Ithacius now wanted all heretics put to death. Martin asked Emperor Maximus to spare the Priscillians and at first he agreed, but as soon as Martin had left the city, he appointed the cruel Prefect Evodius as judge. Evodius decided Priscillian and his friends were guilty of sorcery and in the year 385 he had Priscillian beheaded. Very angry, Martin pleaded yet again for the persecution to cease.

As a result, instead of executing Instantius and Tiberianus, the Emperor banished them to the most remote place he knew. 'Ad Sillivam Insulam ultra Britannicum deportatus'. In the year 387 they were sent to the 'Isle of Scilly'.

So, Martin of Tours saved the lives of Instantius and Tiberianus. The chapel on the headland may have been theirs; perhaps they dedicated it to St Martin in his honour.

That night they stayed in Croker's house. He was a kindly man and they swapped stories till very late.

Next morning by the turf fire they ate porridge.

'Can we repay you for your kindness?' asked Anthony.

'Your company has been payment enough. Travel safely!'

They made their way over to Wine Cove, where a narrow path scrambled down towards the sea. At beach level there was a recess in the cliff from which there was a steady drip of water. A low wall in front contained the water.

'This is Prescella Well,' said Lizzie. 'It's very old. It's the best well on the island; it never dries up.'

'Who was Prescella?'

Then Jamie chimed in, 'Could it be something to do with the bishops in the story, the Priscillians?'

'You never know,' said Anthony, 'you never know.'

To the north-west the beaches of Great Bay gleamed. They swam in the crystal clear water. It was surprisingly cold.

'Don't go out of your depth,' said Lizzie. 'There are some great swimming places here, but near the headlands and in the channels between the islands the currents are strong.'

Then they set off west over Tinkler's Hill in the direction of Lower Town. To the north the moorland stretched to Top Rock Hill, and beyond it a causeway led across to White Island. All around was the sound of the sea.

Soon they were overlooking the bright waters of Teän Sound.

THE KELP BURNERS

'What are you looking at?' Honor Trinder had joined them.

'This pit,' said Jamie. 'Is it a grave?'

Above the low cliffs was a hollow about 5ft across and 2ft deep, neatly lined with granite slabs.

''Tis a pit for burning kelp,' Honor said. 'Almost every family has one.'

'Kelp?'

'Seaweed. Ore-weed they call it.'

'Why do you burn it?'

'It turns into soda ash; people use it to make glass an' soap. Mixed with fat it's a salve for cuts an' sores.'

'How do you know?'

'My familials brought the kelping here in 1684. They tried Falmouth first, but there wasn't much weed an' the cliffs were steep. But here the shallow water is perfect for the weed an' it's easy to gather. ''Twas my great, great granfer James Nance, his wife Susannah an' their sons Henry an' William. They built our cottage on Teän, by the old chapel. No one else would live there. It was too small to farm, too exposed for fishing, but it was great for ore-weed.

'In spring, after a gale the weed is thick on the shore. All the familials help, cutting it off the rocks an' raking it in from the surf. We leave it above high water to start drying. The weed stem is the best bit. In May the long leaves grow. This "May-wrack" isn't as good as the stem, but it all helps. 'Tis hard work. Three hundred pound gathered makes a hundred to burn.

'To finish drying we pile the weed in stooks or hang it on walls. On Teän we have a south-facing wall that's ideal. Then in June we move back into the cottage. If need be the pits are repaired. The men put iron bars across them. The little 'uns fetch furze an' bracken.

'Burning day is jus' like hell! We start before dawn. We burn the furze an' bracken in the pit till the rocks are glowing; then the ore-weed is laid over the iron bars. As the fire burns through more weed is added, criss-cross, til it's all gone. All over the islands there are great columns of white smeech*. It's niffy as anything! The cold ash is solid an' as heavy as granite. We break it into foot-square blocks with

---

*   Smeech: acrid smoke.

crowbars. Each slab is a hundredweight. We take them St Mary's, then they're shipped on to Bristol or Gloucester.

'Scilly is the best place in the world for kelp. ''Tis a good living but it's a pity it's seasonable. The rest of the year we farm an' fish an' row the gig, the worse for us. But now, why don't you come into Lower Town an' meet my familials?'

So they did, and they all told stories late into the starry night.

MAROONED

The mist was thick; no sooner had the lookout shouted to the helmsman than there was the sickening sound of timbers splitting and seams cracking. The barque came to an abrupt halt. Moments later the backstay parted and the rig collapsed over the leeward side of the bow. For a few seconds the waves pounded the broken hull against the cruel rocks. Then with a sickening groan it slid back under the waves.

The voyage from Demerara had been slow, beset with headwinds and storms, then the Western Approaches had been fog-bound. The crew was utterly lost and hungry, too. Of the eighteen men, five now found themselves cast up on an inhospitable shore, lucky to be alive.

There was an Englishman, a Pole, and three Russians. All were soaked, chilled, hungry and weak. At first they rejoiced to be alive. But as night came their spirits fell.

Next morning the mist was no less; visibility was only a few feet. Bower, the Englishman, set off to explore, following the coast. He passed a narrow inlet, wondering if it might once have been used as a landing place, a dark, dripping cave, a point of rocks, a sunken ledge jutting into the sea. After half an hour he was back where he started. It seemed they were marooned on a small, rocky island. They were cold, starving, and had no idea where they were. The mist meant there was no way to summon help and no prospect of rescue or escape.

Once someone thought they heard a dog, but decided it was probably a seal barking. After a second night of fitful sleep they realised they could easily die there. Every hour they grew hungrier and weaker. The constant damp and cold sapped their strength. Delirium was not far off. Once Bower dreamed of a human voice, but there was nothing and no one to be seen, only the mist. Sheltered in the lee of the rocks they began the third night.

Next morning, mist still blanketed the world. Shivering uncontrollably, they realised they could soon be dead.

'I am hungry,' said the Pole. 'You are hungry. Soon we will all die, unless one dies to save the others.'

There was a murmur of agreement. Then the Pole drew his knife. The others drew knives by way of protection.

'In that case,' said the Englishman, 'let us draw lots.'

There were mutters of agreement. One Russian found a sodden pack of cards in his pocket.

'The one who draws the lowest card shall die,' he said, and so it was agreed.

They each took a card. The Pole drew the ten of spades. The Russians in turn drew a king, a seven, and the three of clubs. The last of them crossed himself and prayed aloud. After a brief pause the Englishman drew the two of hearts.

A knife was placed at the Englishman's throat.

'Let it be done quickly,' said the Pole. 'It is most humane.'

'Please,' said the Englishman. 'If you could give me a moment I would like to pray for forgiveness for my sins.'

'You are a coward!'

'Yes I am,' said the Englishman. 'But if I'm providing the supper then you might at least let me say the grace.'

Reluctantly the others agreed. The Englishman prayed.

The Pole waxed poetic: 'The sea is singing a funeral hymn.'

His friends were prosaic: 'Now! The Englishman must die.'

Each man drew his knife and they gathered around the Englishman. One prepared to slit his throat.

Suddenly there was a movement, a sound above the voices of wind and sea.

As one they turned. Amazingly, wonderfully, there stood a figure clad in oilskins and sea boots. They were saved!

The newcomer saw four men turn towards him, all holding knives. He screamed, turned and fled into the mist.

They chased him with all the speed they could muster. The stranger fled as fast as he could from his knife-wielding pursuers. They called for him to stop, in Polish and Russian.

Then, apparently desperate, the poor man ran into the sea.

But the waters did not engulf him. He ran along the ledge of rock Bower had seen two days earlier, but then they followed him onto a sand bar beyond it and land beyond that.

Then, exhausted, he collapsed on the ground.

'I can't go a step further,' he said. 'Kill me if you must.'

'For God's sake,' said Bower, also exhausted. 'We mean no harm. Where did you come from? What land is this?'

'This is the island of St Martin's, one of the Isles of Scilly. I just walked across the causeway to White Island at low tide, to look for wood and to check my curlew traps. Then you chased me with knives. But I have nothing you can steal.'

'Good God! All the time we have been linked to the land by a tidal causeway. When I passed it two days ago it was at half tide and the visibility was only feet.'

'You don't mean to kill me?'

'No, you are our salvation, and I in particular am very grateful for your appearance.'

They made their way to Lower Town. Kind islanders gave them food and drink. Dry clothes were found. Someone discovered a bottle of brandy. The pack of cards was dried carefully, but no one wanted to play.

THE MONSTER OF WHITE ISLAND

'Of course, young Jamie, you should never go near White Island at night. You should warn others to stay away, too.'

The speaker was a weather-beaten sailor.

'Especially, at low water, on a night when there is no moon.

'Some call it Bucca Dhu, others call it Bucca Boo. It's not like the Bucca Gwyn over at Peninnis: that's quite friendly. No, this Bucca is a nasty piece of work. Many's the unsuspecting man that's been dragged down to the depths of its cave, gasping in vain for air, pleading hopelessly for mercy, never to be seen again.'

Jamie looked wide-eyed at Lizzie.

'Don't worry,' she whispered. 'They tell the story to keep people away, specially the excise. On White Island there's a cave at the head of the inlet called Underland Girt. When the moon and tide are right, the free-traders use it as a temporary hiding place.'

SHOES IN THE CHIMNEY

Outside the wind moaned and the ever-present sound of the sea grew louder. The slates rattled and a door banged.

'The sea is a cruel mistress. There isn't a family on the islands hasn't lost a father, a husband or a son to the waves. There's a fair few shoes left in the chimneys of Scilly! Sailors leave them there to ensure a safe return, but too often they remain unclaimed.

'Only a generation back we lost two boats from St Martin's. Terrible it was. But ever since, when it's dark or misty, people often hear the tramp of sea boots coming up the path from Bab's Carn to Lower Town. But when they open their door there's never anyone in sight. They say 'tis the lost spirits making their landfall, again and again until judgement day.'

Jamie shivered and pulled his coat tight about him. Then the next tale began.

CALM

'The wind is dropping,' said Wilkins the mate.

It was a shame, he thought, the passage from Dublin had been safe and swift.

'We must allow for the tide,' said Andrews, the captain.

'Aye, captain,' was the reply.

Andrews continued, 'To the south the flood tide sets toward Wolf Rock, to the west the flood sets among the Isles of Scilly, on the west coast of Cornwall it has an easterly drift. That's why our course takes us close to the Isles of Scilly.'

They looked south-east, where breakers showed the position of the infamous Seven Stones Reef, 2 miles of jagged rock, only visible at half tide.

'Spring tides run at over 2 knots,' added Andrews.

Starboard of the bow lay the Isles of Scilly. The day mark of St Martin's Island was just visible.

Although their speed through the water was almost imperceptible, the islands would pass clear to the west. However, the Seven Stones Reef was now noticeably closer.

'Two points to starboard Mr Wilkins, and all the sail we can muster!' ordered Andrews. For twenty minutes the crew hurried to deploy every possible sail. But even as they hoisted the last topsail, the wind faded to nothing and the canvas hung limply.

Andrews checked the compass. The bearing of the Seven Stones was unchanged; the tide was setting them directly towards the reef. A grim silence descended on the ship.

'We could try rowing,' said the mate. He nodded towards the boat, then, sighing, he shook his head. The schooner was fully laden. The reef extended a mile either side of their course. Four men could not tow her clear.

The swell was breaking over the rocks ahead. The wind had died but the waves, the backwash, the pull and heave retained all the momentum of the Atlantic Ocean. The crew knew that they could not avoid the reef. They looked at the captain.

Launching the boat in the turbulent water near the reef would be dangerous. Every moment they drifted closer and closer.

With a heavy heart he ordered, 'Launch the boat.'

Efficiently, but with a natural reluctance, they swung the boat over the side and lowered it. Taking only a few essentials, they clambered into the tiny craft.

The breakers were now perilously close. They rowed a dozen strokes clear, unwilling to leave the scene and begin the 7-mile row to the Isles of Scilly. All were downcast.

Then, the schooner reached the troubled waters near the reef, pitching and rolling in the swell. The relentless tide pushed her inexorably towards her doom. The end seemed near.

Still the ship was as stately as a queen: the sails a picturesque silhouette. Yet destruction was just yards away. The men could not bear to watch and they could not bear to turn aside.

Then the schooner's forward motion paused. The ship hesitated on the brink of destruction.

'It's the backwash from the reef,' said the mate. 'She could be like that for minutes, but she'll go down just the same.'

'Perhaps the tide has turned,' suggested one of the sailors.

'Not for three hours,' said Wilkins.

In the stern sat Andrews, pale faced, gazing at his boots. He wished he could pay for his error of judgement and go down with his ship.

Then a breath of wind rippled across the sea, stirring the blue expanse, sweeping down from the north-east. The captain felt the breeze on his cheek and looked up at his ship. Slowly her head came round. Then the sails of the schooner filled and slowly but steadily she began sailing away from the rocks.

'Good Lord,' exclaimed Wilkins, 'I wish we were on b …'

'Pull away,' ordered Andrews. 'With a will.'

Swiftly they plied the oars. But it seemed the schooner was fixed on her course to the south. All her sails were set, the breeze was freshening and the ship was leaving them behind.

They grunted with the effort. They cursed the deceitful wind. Before they would have been seen as unfortunate; now they would be a laughing-stock. The ship was no closer.

Then the wind freshened still more; the men groaned. But then the ship turned starboard, rounding up to windward, nearly reaching stays.

'Now, we have her!' The men rowed with renewed vigour. But when they were just yards away the bow came round; she paid off from the wind and started to sail again.

They cried out in frustration. In that little boat every muscle ached, every back was sore, every hand was blistered, every eye stung with sweat.

'Pull on lads,' said Andrews, 'or else it's Scilly for us.'

The schooner sailed magnificently for another minute. Then another gust saw her round up to windward again.

With a mighty effort they drew alongside. Wilkins grabbed a trailing rope. The rowers gave a brief cheer. Andrews swarmed on board and ran to the wheel. Swiftly the rest climbed up. The effort over, the hands laughed with relief.

'Nice breeze,' said Wilkins.

'We must allow for the tide,' said Andrews, the captain.

'Aye, captain,' was the reply.

Soon the Seven Stones were far astern.

NORTHERN
ISLANDS

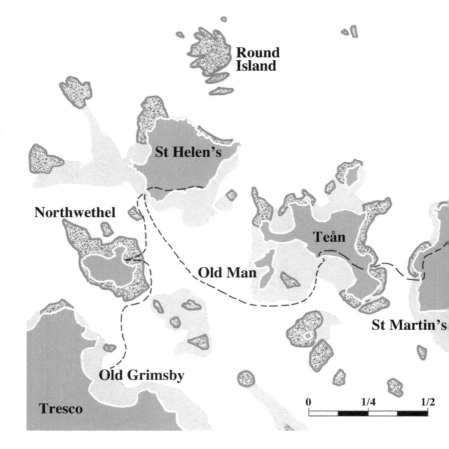

Round
Island

St Helen's

Northwethel

Teån

Old Man

St Martin's

Old Grimsby

Tresco

0   1/4   1/2

6

HWEGH

THE NORTHERN ISLANDS

The Northern Islands are witness to the stormy temporality of their world. Every spring sees one less blade of grass. Swift currents harry the land towards the past.

KELP WARS

Next day Lizzie went to fetch her boat from Cruther's Quay. As Honor rowed Anthony and Jamie over to Teän, she said, 'At low water you can see old walls – they are a thousand years old.'

Ashore they were soon walking on the springy turf above East Porth. Ahead was the Nances' cottage and the remains of the ancient chapel of St Theona.

Honor talked about her family with pride: 'They lived here for three generations, but 'tis only a small island an' by 1750 they were that many that Granfer James motivated to Lower Town on St Martin's. But he still paid the rent for Teän. They would row over to harvest the ore-weed an' at burning time.

'But because Granfer weren't there permanent, that was the cause of the kelp wars. In 1758 he looked out the window an' saw four boats rowing out to Teän from Tresco. Granfer an' his brothers sculled over an' found Robert Jenkin an' five of his men stealing our weed. Caught red-handled they were!

'But the Caterpillars were all ashore, so Granfer untied their boats. They waded out to try an' stop them, but our lads walloped them with their oars. Mighty angry they were, hollerin' an' shouting! Granfer towed the boats back to St Martin's an' left the Caterpillars soaking wet and stranded. Unfortunately, they got rescued next day.

'Then they wanted their boats back, but Granfer wouldn't let 'em go. "Accessories after the fact" he called them. He hid 'em in the bracken on Tinkler's Hill. Next year the council made him give the boats back, more's the pity. But the Caterpillars kept their thieving hands off our weed after that. Granfer Nance was king of the kelp!

'Next generation it happened again. In 1787 my dad saw three Gunnicks paddling out to the island. Gunnicks! From St Martin's, our own island: Thomas Woodcock, his son an' James Ashford! We caught 'em red-handled too, so Dad took 'em to the twelve men of Scilly an' they fined 'em 2s 6d each for trespassing on our preservatives.

'Serve 'em right I say! An' that was the end of the Kelp Wars.'

'Why are people from Tresco called Caterpillars?' asked Anthony, but no one seemed to know.

ST HELEN'S

Then there was a friendly shout from the water's edge – it was Lizzie. 'Come on,' she said. 'Let's go to St Helen's.'

Fondly they bade farewell to Honor and soon they were sailing round the carn called Old Man.

'There's a druid grave there,' said Lizzie.

'A Bronze Age entrance tomb,' translated Anthony.

'They found treasure,' said Lizzie. 'Brooches and things.'

South of St Helen's Lizzie announced, 'This is St Helen's Pool. It used to be the main anchorage for all the islands. The Tresco monks collected tolls from the ships anchored here.'

'Who was St Helen?' asked Jamie.

Lizzie looked blank and Anthony answered.

'No one really knows why St Helen's has its name. It used to be the home of a holy person called St Lide.*

'No one knows why the name changed. It could have just gradually altered: Lide, Elid, Eled, Elen, Helen. Or maybe the dedication changed after the Reformation. Neither explanation is very convincing.'

'But who was Helen anyway?' asked Lizzie.

'We have three choices,' said Anthony. 'Helen, Empress of Constantinople, mother of Constantine the Great, or Helen of Caernarfon, or it could be someone local.'

THE PEST HOUSE

As Jamie pondered this inconclusive answer, Lizzie suddenly called out, 'No flag, no flag!'

Jamie looked at her quizzically.

'That building, that's the Pest House. If the Yellow Jack is flying, we have to stay away, or we get foreign diseases.'

As the little ship drew up to a quay in front of the building, Anthony nodded, 'A Yellow Jack means "Q" for quarantine.'

'Quite right, sir!' It was the young naval surgeon lieutenant who ran the quarantine station. He took the painter and made it fast. Clearly, he was pleased to have some company.

'Officially this is St Helen's Isolation Hospital, unofficially it's the Pest House. Built to replace the *Pandora*, the hospital ship that used to anchor here. Any plague-ridden ship heading for England must first call here. It's not allowed to move until it's been clear of infection for forty days.

'This building is where we treat them and this graveyard is where we bury them! Come and have a cup of tea!'

Over tea Anthony told a story called 'The Sailor's Tragedy'.

Once there was a loose-living young sailor. He inveigled two young ladies and both of them ended up expecting a child by him. He

---

*   Also known as Elid or Elidius.

married one of them, but the other went and hanged herself rather than suffer the shame of having a fatherless child. But before she hanged herself, she swore that she would have revenge on that young man.

From that moment her ghost haunted him day and night. He could get no rest and back luck came to everything he tried. Eventually he could stand it no more so he fled back to the sea. There he thought he was safe.

Well, one day his ship was becalmed near the Isles of Scilly. That sailor was at the topmast looking for wind, when over the ocean he saw a small boat approaching and in it was the ghost. He climbed down and begged the captain to hide him. The captain agreed so the sailor went and hid in the hold.

The ghost reached the ship. 'Cap'n,' she demanded. 'You have a sailor on this ship that I have come to claim. You must hand him over to me.'

'I can't do that,' said the captain. 'He was ill so we took him to St Helen's, to the pest house, and there he died.'

'Captain, you are lying. I know he is on this ship. Unless you give him to me, I shall call up a storm that will sink you all.'

So, to save his ship and the rest of his men, the captain went below, seized that young sailor and gave him to the ghost.

'I have you now!' she said, and the trembling sailor was forced into her boat.

As the captain and his men looked on there was a great flash of fire and the ghost, her boat and the sailor vanished from this world on a voyage to hell!

Lizzie grinned from ear to ear.

ST HELEN'S HERMITAGE

'Of course,' said the lieutenant, 'there were people here long before the Navy. In the south-east corner of the island was the home of St Lide, who was a bishop and a saint.

'At first, in the eighth century, it was just a hermitage, with one little round hut and an oratory. But in time they built huts for visitors. They grew their own food as well.

'By the eleventh century they had a little church and in 1120 it was granted to Tavistock Abbey. They made a grand shrine for St Lide out of Purbeck marble, and pilgrims came from miles away.

'In those days the sea was not so high and on 8 August each year, the feast of St Lide, the monks from Tresco would process across the downs and over a causeway to the island.'

'Could Lide have been a heretic, a Priscillian?'

'I doubt it. The Priscillians were fourth century but the earliest remains here are eighth century. It's unlikely the heresy would have been maintained for 400 years.'

THE TINNER'S REST

'I can tell you something about Lide,' said Anthony.

The lieutenant looked surprised.

'In tin-mining areas they called March Lide month.

'The first Friday in March was Lide's day. In those days children worked down the mines and on Lide's day the youngest miner was sent on to the highest waste tip of the tin work and allowed to sleep there as long as he could. The length of his sleep was then used as the duration of the afternoon nap for his fellow tinners for the next year.

'Of course, the weather on the first Friday in March was unlikely to be conducive to sleep in an exposed place! And no record has ever been found of any miner getting an afternoon nap at work! It's probably just a tinners' joke, but they still remember it in Cornwall.'

THE TALE OF OLAF TRIGGVASON

Olaf Triggvason was a Viking born in about 960. He was expert at piracy and plunder. But in 986 when sailing south of Ireland, Olaf remembered a tale of a seer on the Isles of Scilly: a hermit famous for piety, learning and knowledge. Olaf was filled with curiosity. He wondered if the seer could foretell his future, so he anchored nearby.

To test the seer, Olaf dressed one of his men in kings' clothes and sent him in his place. But the seer told the servant, 'You are no king and my advice to you is to be loyal to he who is your king.'

When Olaf heard what had happened he was sure that the seer was indeed powerful and wise. He went to him and asked about his future. The seer said, 'You will become a famous king and do famous deeds. You will bring many to faith and baptism, to the good of yourself and many more.'

But then the seer went on, 'So you may have no doubt, I will also tell you this. When returning to your ship you will be ambushed. There will be a battle, you will lose some of your men and you will be wounded. At the point of death, you will be carried to your ship on a shield. But within seven days you will be healed and soon after you will be baptised.'

Olaf returned to his ships and as foretold there was an ambush and a fierce battle. Several men were killed and Olaf himself was wounded. At the point of death he was carried to his ship on a shield, but after seven days he was healed. Olaf was now sure that the holy man of Scilly was a true prophet.

Olaf returned to the seer and asked how he foretold the future. The hermit said that the God of Christian men told him. He told Olaf about his God and Olaf was so impressed he asked to be baptised along with all his men. Olaf studied there a long time and when he left his party included priests and learned men.

Olaf gave up raiding Christian cities, living for many years in England and Ireland. In 995 he returned to Norway. There he found there was a revolt against the king, Haakon Jarl. The king hid from the rebels in a pig sty, but was murdered there by his own slave. Olaf persuaded the rebels to accept him as their leader and so became King of Norway. Later he was confirmed as a Christian by Alphege, Bishop of Winchester. Through King Ethelred he invited bishops and priests to Norway, so making it a Christian country.

No one knows the name of the seer who converted Olaf. It is tempting to think it was St Lide, but no one really knows.

THE INVASION OF NORTHWETHEL

Northwethel, between St Helen's and Tresco, is not the largest of the Isles of Scilly. 300 yards long, 100 yards wide, and 50ft high, it comprises two hills joined by a lower stretch of land.

In the Civil War, Parliament sent Sir Robert Blake to take control of the islands. Rather than risk a frontal assault on St Mary's and its castles, he decided to invade Tresco first and use it as a base for further operations. Led by Colonel Bawden, the Roundheads* tried to land at New Grimsby, but were driven back into the sea. Having regrouped, Blake then positioned his ships north and east of Tresco. At night, with muffled oars, 1,500 men were ferried ashore in forty small boats. They consolidated a position on the beachhead and raised a defensive enclosure around it.

They seemed to have surprised the Royalists for there was no sign of opposition. Colonel Bawden sent two soldiers up the hill above the landing sight to see if the enemy was visible. After thirty minutes they had not returned. The colonel then sent two more with instructions to take particular care. After another thirty minutes they too had not returned. Suspecting a trap, the colonel dispatched two full platoons up the hill under the command of his best officer. On the far side of the hill they found the original four soldiers, sitting in the ground, helpless with both mirth and frustration. There was not a Royalist in sight.

However, ahead of them was the Old Grimsby Channel with Tresco beyond it. Rather than attacking Tresco, they had invaded Northwethel by mistake, where the main opposition were some rather truculent sheep.

The Royalists told everyone it was a precautionary landing, necessary because the Old Grimsby Channel was too rough. Some blamed a local pilot by the name of Nance for misleading them. But Islanders know the true story! Still, a day later Blake tried again and that time he got it right.

---

*   Parliamentarian soldiers.

⟨⟩

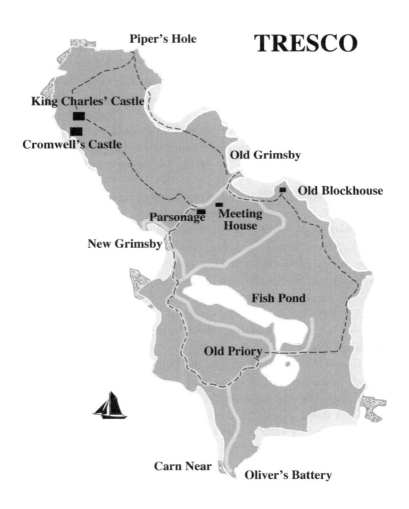

Piper's Hole

TRESCO

King Charles' Castle

Cromwell's Castle

Old Grimsby

Old Blockhouse

Parsonage Meeting
House

New Grimsby

Fish Pond

Old Priory

Carn Near

Oliver's Battery

0   1/4   1/2

7

SEYTH

TRESCO

Once the largest of the islands, joined to Bryher and Samson, Tresco
was the land of the ancient tinners, the king's forest of Guffaer, the
sacred groves of Avallen, woods of elder, of red and roe deer and wild
boar, of prior and priest, of myth and legend. Now it has a remembered
sanctity, an echo of Eden.

THE ISLAND OF TRESCO

It was only a short sail from St Helen's Pool to Tresco.

Anthony was in his element: 'The old name for Tresco, Bryher and
Samson was Renteman or Ryn Tewyn. It's Cornish for promontory of
sand dunes, which suggests that they were then part of the island of
Ennor. The name could be 2,000 years old. By the time of the Priory it
was called St Nicholas Island. But in medieval times it was also called
Trescau and Iniscaw: farmstead or island of elder trees. The monks
used Latin but the islanders spoke Cornish.'

The little boat slipped into Old Grimsby harbour.

'Why is it called Grimsby?' asked Jamie,. 'That's a place in Lincolnshire.'

'It is, but the letter 'b' has only appeared recently. The name
was given by Vikings. It used to be called Old Grymsey, Viking for
Grymr's island. Grymr was one of Odin's names; it means "the mask".
He was always using disguises.'

They left the boat safely moored by the slipway and, watched by the new moon, they slept on the shore in a tent made from the yard and sail.

Next day they followed a track south-east. South of the harbour was a small fort on a knoll.

'That's Dover Fort,' said Lizzie. 'But we just call it the old block-house. In the Civil War Colonel Wogan was in charge.'

'Edward Wogan!' Anthony took up the tale. 'The hero of the siege of Duncannon and saviour of Waterford: a real thorn in Cromwell's side. But here he was outnumbered. Even so, he initially repelled the Parliamentarians, but then he was shot in the foot and had to surrender. General Blake gave him the choice of joining the king's allies in Scotland or retiring to the country. He went north to fight for his king.'

TRESCO MONASTERY

They continued along the coast path and soon passed a large lake that nearly bisected the island.

'The herons love it. It's called the fish pond, but it's best known for its eels,' said Lizzie. 'You know, it's the only freshwater lake in the Isles of Scilly.'

Anthony looked bemused. 'Back in the sixth century there were Celtic churchmen here. They left stone-lined graves and a memorial stone. Then in AD 946, Benedictine monks founded a little monastery; it was dedicated to St Nicholas.'

'Who was St Nicholas?' asked Jamie. Lizzie knew.

ST NICHOLAS

Nicholas lived in Myra in Asia Minor in the fourth century.[*] He had a rich inheritance and was very kind; he helped the poor and gave secret gifts to people in need.

---

[*]   Now Demre in south-west Turkey.

There once was a merchant who had fallen on hard times; he had three daughters.

When the eldest daughter wanted to get married, she could not as her father did not have enough money for a dowry. So one night Nicholas secretly dropped a bag of gold down the chimney. The girl had been washing her stockings and had hung them by the fire to dry. The bag of gold fell into one of the stockings, so she could get married after all.

Later, the middle daughter wanted to get married, but her father still did not have enough for a dowry. Again, Nicholas dropped a bag of gold down the chimney. Again the bag fell into a stocking that the daughter had hung by the fire to dry, so she too could get married.

Eventually the youngest daughter wanted to get married. Her father hid by the fire every evening. When the gold fell into the stocking he ran outside and found it was Nicholas. Nicholas begged him not to tell anyone. But soon the news got out and when anyone received a secret gift they suspected it was from Nicholas. For his generosity he was made a saint.

Because many secret gifts are given at Christmas, they were often attributed to 'Santa Niklaus', often shortened to Santa Claus. Christmas stockings are hung in the hope of his gifts, just like in the story.

'But why would they celebrate Nicholas here?'

'Easy. St Nicholas is also the patron saint of sailors!'

Once Nicholas sailed on a pilgrimage to the Holy Land. A great storm rose up and in the midst of it Nicholas saw the devil clamber on board, intending to sink the ship. The pilgrims were in despair, but Nicholas calmed the waves by his prayers and all were saved.

On another occasion a ship was driven into shallow water and grounded. The sailors prayed for help. To their surprise a figure appeared on the ship and helped them. As soon as the boat was free the figure vanished.

Safe ashore, the sailors looked for a church where they could thank God for their rescue. There they recognised Bishop Nicholas as the man who helped them.

That's why the Sailors' Prayer is 'May St Nicholas hold the tiller'.

TRESCO PRIORY

As they approached the walls of the old priory grounds they noticed movement. A figure was surreptitiously slipping a small parcel through a hole at the base of the wall. Lizzie started loudly whistling a popular tune and the figure, a clergyman, stood and surveyed the view. He looked flustered.

'Hello, Lizzie, I just dropped my pipe you know.'

'Of course,' said Lizzie. 'Mr Evans, these are my friends Jamie and Anthony. Anthony is blind.'

'Oh how unfortunate.' The clergyman breathed a sigh of relief. He reached out and shook Anthony's hand. 'Evans, David Evans, I'm the Missioner for Tresco and Bryher. Have you come to look at the ruins?'

'Yes,' interjected Lizzie, pointedly, 'That's all we are interested in.'

As they walked on towards the ruins of the priory church, Jamie quickly glanced in the hole in the wall. Inside was a stone-lined chamber and there several parcels were hidden. Then Jamie joined the others, his exploit unnoticed.

The priory ruins overlooked the south-east end of the fish pool. They were in a sad state. There was no roof; two arches remained intact, but the walls were largely broken down.

The building had been about 90ft by 30, the size of a small Cornish parish church.

The Missioner was keen to establish his credentials: 'The old monastery was refounded as the Priory of St Nicholas in about 1120 when King Henry I granted the land to "Osbert, Abbot of Tavistock and Turold", his monk. I expect Turold was the senior monk here. Pope Celestine III endorsed it in 1193.

'Now it's sad. The doors, windows and transept arches were made with beautiful, fine-grained, red stone from Normandy. The roof was supported on stout timbers. To the south other buildings served as refectory, library and accommodation.'

'Cloisters?' asked Anthony.

'I don't think so,' said Evans. 'The Priory just had a handful of monks, at times perhaps just one or two. It never had an abbot, which tells us there weren't more than twelve monks, so it never was an abbey, though some call it that. The nearest abbot was at its "parent" church, Tavistock Abbey.

'I'm afraid the Priory had a troubled history. In the fourteenth century pirates almost destroyed it and took everything valuable. Leyland called it "a poor celle of monkes".

'Of course, the Priory did not survive the Dissolution of the Monasteries. It may have closed earlier. The people here lost their church and an important employer.

'The frustrating thing is that small churches were later built on St Agnes and St Martin's, and the church on St Mary's was largely rebuilt, too, but Tresco was left with just a ruin.

'My dad says the Priory was plundered at the Reformation and burned during the Civil War,' said Lizzie.

'Yes, at some time the church was burned,' agreed Evans. 'In about 1782, a man clearing the west end found a large piece of a bombshell and bits of coked timber. No damage is remembered in recent generations, so the fire probably happened in the Civil War.

'Then the ruins were used as improvised dwellings and the church was robbed of stone and timber. But people here still believe the ground is holy. They use the grounds and the church itself as a burial ground.'

'I can tell you a legend or two about this place!' said a new voice from the bushes.

They were abruptly joined by another clergyman. He could not wait to speak and without introduction he began his tale.

THE LEGEND OF THE KNIGHT
AND THE DWARF

One May morning in the mid-fourteenth century the abbey was all confusion as local people sought refuge there, full of fear. The Abbot was beside himself, aimlessly calling 'Monseigneur St Nicholas come to our aid,' and lamenting the absence of the warrior Bras-de-fer and his men.

The abbey was threatened by rentiers: mercenaries and robbers. Their terms were submit or die, and their advanced parties were already on Bryher Hill.

Gloomily an old captain posted a handful of troops to the best advantage and sent the non-combatants out of the way. But then a joyful shout was heard: Bras-de-fer! The warrior had arrived at last but, alas, he had arrived alone.

Worse still, he then told the Abbot that the leader of the rentiers was a devil incarnate, Jean l'Ecorcheur, one who flayed his captives alive.

The Abbot protested the absence of Bras-de-fer's men, 'The church grants you land on condition you come to her aid!'

Bras-de-fer was not roused. 'My wife, Lady Claude, is in labour. I could not move her here nor could I leave her unguarded at home. To defend her and the castle of Ennor, I left my men, but here I came myself, as bound in honour, to fight, and, if need be, to die in your service.'

The Abbot groaned. 'Aways, a woman is at the bottom of evil or mischance. As they say, *ubi foemina, ibi diabolus!** Of course, you are right. But I wish that your fair wife had chosen her time better. She is a woman, and it is ill dealing with that troublesome sex.'

Frowning at these words, Bras-de-fer took command. All who could bear arms were mustered in divisions, led by veteran soldiers. Archers and crossbow men were sent to the walls. Preparations were made for pouring molten pitch and boiling water onto the enemy. The drawbridge was raised and between it and the gate was built a

---

*   Where there is a woman, there is the devil!

breastwork the height of a man's shoulders and defended by ten picked crossbow men. The best troops were held in reserve in the courtyard.

Then Bras-de-fer ordered a manchet of bread and beef with a good black jack of humming ale for every man.* He urged all to acquit themselves as men and faithful servants of the Church.

Soon a daunting scene met their eyes. Before them gathered a vast body of men, marshalled in several divisions. They were preceded by bowmen who acted as scouts. At the head, clad in steel, rode L'Ecorcheur.

Two bowshots from the Abbey they halted. Then, advancing a few paces nearer, L'Ecorcheur demanded all to surrender or face, 'Death to all within the walls and for your leader, a higher bough for hanging.'

'Thank you for your courtesy, Sir Rentier,' said Bras-de-fer. 'The walls of St Nicholas are high and his servants bold, so we will defend our holy Church. The more readily, too, since we do not trust a word you say!

'Now, Sir Flayer, retire. If you stay where you are, we will try the quality of your armour. Shoot, men, shoot!'

It was as well that l'Ecorcheur took Bras-de-fer's advice. He was unharmed, but two arrows struck his horse, which bounded furiously and nearly dismounted him. He gave orders to attack.

Men advanced bearing pavises, tall shields. Behind each followed an archer or crossbow man, looking for a chance to fire at those manning the walls. Several moveable towers followed; then mangonels, machines for throwing large stones. A sharp exchange continued for nearly half an hour, then there was a pause. Both sides assessed their casualties.

The result was in favour of the Abbey. No one on the walls had been hurt. Two or three non-combatants had been touched by spent shafts, but there were no serious casualties. Nearly a dozen besiegers had been killed or badly injured.

Jean L'Ecorcheur foamed with rage. He shook his clenched fist at the Abbey and shouted blasphemies at its guardians. He ordered his men to attack again. Long ladders were prepared and brought to the front, while a fresh band of archers came forward and watched every

---

*   Manchet: small loaf, black jack: leather tankard, humming ale: strong beer.

portion of the walls. But Bras-de-fer too was not idle, moving from post to post, advising, cautioning and motivating. At last, he reached a corner tower, where the Abbot looked on.

'What think you, Sir Bras-de-fer?'

'They have gained nothing, but they have lost some of their best men. But what is this?'

He pointed to a figure on the ramparts. It was the Abbot's favourite dwarf dragging, with difficulty, an antique weapon of enormous size and weight. The Abbot was indignant.

'That profane imp has laid his sacrilegious hands upon the bow of blessed St Nicholas! It belonged to a Cornish giant who robbed pilgrims coming to the abbey. Our saint took it from the heathen and slew him with his own weapon. You misshapen knave, don't you know the sanctity of that consecrated weapon?'

'Do you not know, Lord Abbot,' replied the dwarf, 'that a bolt from this can pierce chain mail at 500 paces?'

To the smiles of Bras-de-fer and the wrath of the Abbot, he dragged the great bow to the parapet. He tried to string it, but in vain. The bow and cord, as if of steel, resisted his efforts.

Then the enemy attack restarted, more vigorous than ever. Jean l'Ecorcheur spotted the Abbot in his place of safety. Wild with rage, he shouted abuse at the Abbey and its occupants. Standing in his stirrups, he demanded the defenders yield.

'You dog of an Abbot!' he cried, 'for the slaughter of my men, I will roast together, in a slow fire, you and the image of your mock saint, Nicholas, whom may Beelzebub ...'

The sentence was never completed.

Bras-de-fer had watched the dwarf's abortive efforts to bend the mighty bow of St Nicholas. Then, easing the little man gently aside, he took the cord and drew it to the spring. He placed a bolt in the groove and took aim. As l'Ecorcheur was pouring out his blasphemies, the bow of St Nicholas avenged him. The bolt entered his mouth and passed into his brain. The rentier sprang convulsively into the air and fell lifeless on the ground. Bras-de-fer signalled his men to cease fire.

There was a rush to the spot where the body lay, but then the host melted away. Soon not a rentier was left on Tresco.

The Abbot was relieved and happy. Bras-de-fer lamented he had not had the honour of defeating his foe in single combat, but the Abbot countered him.

'You are right,' replied Bras-de-fer, 'And our little friend deserves more credit than I. God gave him the idea. He conceived, I only executed. Thus God rebukes our pride, for He made Bras-de-fer second to this feeble child. It is God who is our Deliverer. To Him and to His Name, be praise!'

The story completed, its teller triumphantly introduced himself: 'Whitfield, Reverend Henry Whitfield.'

DICK THE WICKED

Below the ruins of the priory were tumbledown cottages.

Whitfield continued, 'I tell you the recent inhabitants of these cottages make a sad contrast with the good people that lived here in the days of the Abbey.

'Not long ago one of them was a man pre-eminent in wickedness – even in times of piracy and plunder – and known for his ability to see the supernatural.

'This man was "Dick the Wicked", who cared nothing for the place he lived nor its history. Always recognisable by his long loose coat, he spent his time in wrecking, plundering and other lawless deeds, even though he lived on holy ground.

'Dick, it was said, was a man who defied all agencies: human, diabolical and divine.'

Once there was a poor shipwrecked Dutchman. He was murdered and buried in a sandbank near Tresco farm. Most people wouldn't go near there after nightfall. But Dick the Wicked had no such scruples. He often saw the ghost of the dead man pacing gloomily up and down at the side of the road, never saying a word. When spoken to, the ghost did not reply, but always moved silently onward, and, at the end of his beat, turned back again. No one else ever saw the figure, nor did they want to, but Dick the Wicked had second sight and feared nothing.

On another occasion, Dick the Wicked was walking over Abbey Hill on the path to the ruins. Suddenly he saw approaching him the apparition of another dead person, someone once well known to him. Now a ghost, on meeting any one, will always pass them on the right and it did so on this occasion. Dick's fiery temper was roused in a moment. 'What!' he said, 'How dare you take my right side!' The ghost did not answer this bold challenge, but turned and followed him all the way home. Unperturbed, Dick went inside and locked the door and the ghost vanished away.

Now Dick and his old henchman, Johnny, had shared many wild exploits. They agreed that whichever of them died first would come back and tell the other where he was and what it was like.

Well, Johnny died first and Dick the Wicked waited for him to call, but nothing happened. As Dick had second sight and was not scared to converse with ghosts and spirits, he was rather disappointed.

One evening Dick was crossing the burial ground in the ruins, heading towards his cottage. As he did so he remembered Johnny, sleeping quietly under the turf of the graveyard. So as Dick entered his cottage he called out, 'Johnny, Johnny, will you not keep your word?'

But even as Dick spoke, there was a sound like thunder, so terrible that his hair bristled and stood on end and his hat rose up in the air. In that fearful sound, his friend's voice seemed to reply. It shook the walls and the roof until they trembled, but Dick could not make out what Johnny was saying.

Next night the same thing happened. There was the sound like thunder, the shaking walls and roof, the bristling hair, and the fearful voice, but still Dick could not understand.

Next night it was the same again: thunder, shaking, the bristling, the voice, and this time an invisible hand moved Dick's clothes and furniture about.

Every night these visions became more and more terrible, and even Dick the Wicked became frightened. Eventually, when the thunder, the shaking and the voice were at their worst, Dick lay trembling in his bed. The chairs scraped across the floor, the table moved and then the door burst open. In marched a fiendish figure, declaring: 'If thee won't come to me, Dick, then I shall have to take thee.' It strode inside and marched, arms outstretched, towards the bed.

Next morning, Dick was found by his friends, wrapped in his long loose coat a considerable distance from his house. No one knew how he got there. But till the day he died, Dick swore that that Satan himself had tried to carry him away, but had failed in the attempt.

'I'm so wicked that even Old Nick won't have anything to do with me,' he used to say.

THE SON OF WICKED DICK

The only-slightly-less-wicked son of Dick the Wicked was the last of the family with second sight. Dick the Younger was a tall man, also scared of no one, with a fine head of black hair.

One evening, he brought his horse into the abbey grounds to an outbuilding that he used as a stable. He was busy feeding and watering his horse, when he felt the animal suddenly start and tremble violently.

He looked up, and saw, standing on the wall, the figure of a man, pale, grim, and stern. He was wearing old-fashioned clothes and a tricorn hat. The figure gazed at him angrily.

Dick the Younger turned away in terror and, leaving the steed securely tethered, he walked very briskly to his cottage. But the ghost was too much for the poor horse. It gave a jerk and broke its halter. Dick's son was surprised when his horse reached the cottage door at the same time that he did! History does not relate if he let the horse inside.

A REPROOF FOR SCOFFERS

Now you may laugh at the tales of Dick the Wicked and his son. But I advise against it. Remember what it says in the Book of Proverbs: a scoffer is an abomination to men! This is what happened to some scoffers here.

A few years back some young men were strolling among the tombs in the churchyard, joking and scoffing at the experiences of Dick and his son. One young man, either bolder or more foolish than the rest, shouted in defiance of the ghosts that haunted the place. He had just declaimed the words of the first psalm:

As wind blows chaff away,
So, in the presence of the Lord,
The wicked shall decay.

Then there was a clap of thunder right above him. A great gust of wind lifted his hat from his head, whirled it around and dashed it against the wall. In terror the young scoffers ran away as fast as they could!

THE WITCHES' MARK

The clergyman continued with passion. 'Let me warn you, Tresco is a favourite gathering place of witches.'

One evening Dick the Younger was walking out near Tresco Farm. There he saw five ancient crones just as you find depicted in old books. In the moonlight they were doing a devilish dance. They seemed to be riding on sticks placed between their legs, as if they were children's hobby horses.

But the moment Dick stumbled on the witches, he was seen. Straight away the dancing stopped. One of them, who he recognised as a relative, called him by name.

'Young Dick, you go straight home and mind you tell no one what you've seen here tonight, or else you shall wear my mark till your dying day!'

Dick the Younger was filled with terror and promised to tell no one, then he ran home as fast as his legs would carry him.

For a long time he kept the secret, but every day that passed it weighed more heavily on his conscience. At last he could not stop himself from telling his wife what he had seen.

Then he remembered the witch's instruction. Trembling, he waited for some imminent retribution. There was no sound, no motion, nothing. Thinking the moment past, Dick went to bed and slept soundly.

When he woke next day he turned to speak to his wife. She screamed as if she had seen a ghost. Dick the Younger rushed to the mirror. There he saw that the witches, in revenge, had turned his jet black hair white in a single night.

THE BEWITCHED FLOCK

On another occasion, one of the same coven came to the house of a neighbour of Dick the Younger. She was known to Dick and his friend and always wore a little red cloak. She tried to sell the neighbour a sheep and a lamb, but the price was exorbitant, so he refused to buy them. The old woman left, muttering strangely, wrapping her cloak around her.

That evening that poor man went out to his field to find that his choice ram had suddenly died for no apparent reason. Next day another of his flock died. Every day one more sheep died. Soon ruin was staring him in the face. At last, he went off to ask a wise sister what to do. She told him to kindle a huge fire, and to burn the next animal that died.

So he gathered as much kindling and firewood as he could. Sure enough, when he went back to his field, he found yet another sheep was stiff and cold. He lit the fire and put the sheep upon it.

Now he knew that the woman who had tried to sell him the sheep and lamb was at that moment some distance away in her own house, having just returned from New Grimsby. But as the flames blazed up he raised his eyes. On the hedge nearby he saw that very person grinning diabolically, still wrapped in her red cloak. But as the flames rose higher the figure vanished and no more of his flock were lost.

'What do you think of that, boy?' concluded Whitfield.

Jamie was about to speak when a confident voice from behind him said: 'It may be a good story, but it seriously maligns the ladies of Tresco.'

A figure in military uniform stepped from the shadows.

'Heath, Captain Robert Heath.'

'And what do you know about it, Captain?'

'Rather a lot, actually. I know these people very well.'

'So, you too are a devil worshipper?'

'I am a rational observer, not prone to falling for sensationalist stereotypes.'

Whitfield looked angry, 'Then sir, kindly explain your rational self.'

THE WHITE WITCHES OF SCILLY

As an officer at the Garrison it is my job to know these people. Here there is no doctor, dentist, nurse, midwife, or veterinary surgeon. It is the wise women of the islands, especially Tresco, that fulfil those roles.

They often use the term 'Aunt' for the 'wise women' of the community. Two generations ago, Aunt Sarah Jenkins, a notably wise woman, was the leader of what should be called a college of healers, certainly not a coven. She was remarkable for her venerable beard, which some imagined miraculously benefited those that stroked it. Now her descendant Mary Jenkin, known as 'Aunt Polly', has that role. They work to help those in distress for pity's sake rather than profit. They have no ambition to be thought wise, nor do they put on airs and graces to justify a fat fee. They use plain and intelligible English and their sole motivation is to remove pain and procure ease. The patient can seldom persuade them to accept any present until the cure is complete.

They have medicines obtained from surgeons of merchant ships and men-o'-war and sometimes apothecaries. But also they are good

botanists with many herbs in their catalogue, all of which have proved
effective over the centuries. They have some secret cures – the recipes
are held by Aunt Polly.

They have no skeleton to show the articulation of the bones, but
they direct the slipping in of a joint or the mending of a broken limb
by comparing it with its fellow, at the same time applying something
to ease the pain. Wounds are soon cured by their soft bandages and
warm balsams; swellings are soon reduced by their warm poultices.

This kind wisdom is the survival and distillation of ancient
knowledge, not a cult with a priesthood or a coven:

> Here we behold what Doctors ought to be,
> Their practice what, and what should be their fee.
> Taught by Old Women, let them learn their part,
> How much they owe to Nature more than Art.
> The fam'd Hippocrates they never read,
> Galen, nor Boerhaave, Hans Sloane, nor Mead.*
> Dispensaries, the Doctor's last resource,
> Are substituted by a skilful Nurse:
> She ministers, but watches Nature's cue,
> And wise Experience tells her what to do.
> With Simples, or Compounds, as suits the case,
> She moves the Pain, and gives the Patient Ease.
> The Pulse she raises, in low Ebb of Blood,
> And lowers to Order, throbbing at high Flood:
> With Words of Comfort banishes each Fear.
> And friendly soothes away the Patient's Care.
> O mighty Phoebus! if you can, prescribe
> A better Practice for the learned Tribe:
> For which of all ye Sons of Art can vaunt
> The Cures accomplish'd by a Scilly-Aunt?

The amiable verse complete, Heath bade farewell and headed towards
Old Grimsby.

*   All famous physicians.

Whitfield looked taken aback at being contradicted. Then he looked straight at Jamie, 'You believe that, boy?'

Jamie stuttered, uncertain what to say. Anthony began to reply, but Whitfield snorted in disapproval and marched away.

There was an awkward silence. Then Jamie asked, 'Where shall we stay tonight?'

Evans said, 'There's nowhere comfortable here. Why don't you stay at the Mission House? I have plenty of room.'

THE REVEREND SMUGGLERS OF TRESCO

Below his home, Evans showed them the old meeting house: two fishermen's cottages joined to make a hall.*

'It was the only community building after the Priory Church was destroyed. We must build a proper church here one day.'

Then they returned to the Missioner's House, a splendid, double-fronted building looking out to the north-east.

'I'm lucky, it's a fine house, the SPCK had it built specially. The land was leased by the Governor.'

As they were shown around, Jamie noticed the big brass telescope at one of the upstairs windows. On the table were *The New Admiralty Signal-Book for the Ships of War* and *Night Signals and Instructions for the Conduct of Ships of War*. The view out to St Helen's Pool was magnificent.

'I like to watch the ships come and go,' said Evans. 'Like the shepherd watching his flock.'

On the ground floor an open door beneath the stairs showed more steps leading down to cellars.

'Nothing to see down there,' said Evans, quickly shutting the door, 'Let's go to the sitting room and have tea.'

Evans disappeared into the kitchen.

'Don't say a thing,' said Lizzie. 'But everyone here helps with the free trading, even the clergymen. It's the only way we survive. They

---

* St Nicholas' Church was built on the site in 1879.

say that had the King and Queen lived on Scilly, they would have smuggled, just like everyone else.

'But you mustn't ever talk about it. It's not that long since Reverend Troutbeck had to run away when he got found out. They caught him with some smuggled sugar; it was lucky they didn't find anything else. They say he went to Cumbria, which was as far away as he could get.'

THE LEGEND OF THE DANE'S GRAVE

On the mantelpiece were the usual memorabilia and candlesticks. Among them was a perfectly round, smoothed pebble.

Evans explained.

'Not far from here is an ancient grave traditionally known as "The Dane's Grave". When it was excavated, in the centre of the skeleton, where the heart would be, there was this pebble. What did it mean? Was it there by chance? Was it a heart stone? Was it a soul stone? Was is placed there to indicate that the figure once had a heart of stone? Or was that the very stone from a catapult that ended his days, striking a cruel blow to the heart and shocking it into eternal silence?

'To explain this discovery, Whitfield told me a tale about Leofric, supposedly the Abbot of Tresco, and Ulf, a marauding Viking. Ulf attacked Tresco, captured Leofric and brought him back to the Abbey to demand a ransom. But a young monk, copying the shepherd boy David, used a sling. Its stone struck Ulf on the heart and he dropped dead.

'But history knows nothing of Ulf the Dane or Leofric the Abbot of Tresco.

'We know that the Dioceses of Crediton and Cornwall were granted by Edward the Confessor to a Bishop Leofric, probably a native of Cornwall. We also know that a Prior Alan of Tresco was made Abbot of Tavistock in 1233. I think Whitfield made up the story from those little-known facts.'

Next day they wandered down the lane to New Grimsby. Anthony found two fishermen to swap stories with, but Jamie and Lizzie scuttled off to explore the north end of the island.

They walked north on open heath, springy heather and ling, so different from the wooded centre of the island. Looking over to Bryher they could see that its northern part was also heath.

'My mum says it's because there's nothing between it and the north wind,' said Lizzie. 'But Dad says it's where the ice got to, thousands of years ago.'

Ahead they could see a small castle at the water's edge and another dilapidated structure on the hill above.

'The bottom one is Oliver Cromwell's castle, and the top one is King Charles' castle, but neither man ever saw the castle bearing his name.'

THE LEGEND OF KING CHARLES' CASTLE

The castle named after King Charles is from long before his time. It was built in about 1550, to fire on Spanish or French ships trying to enter the channel between Bryher and Tresco.

During the Civil War John Grenville, Governor of Scilly, gave command of King Charles' Castle to William Edgcumb, a brave young man of a noble Cornish family.

His task seemed hopeless. The Protectorate, which had struck down the crown of England, was not likely to be checked by a handful of zealous men on a distant isle.

But though there was little chance of victory, there was honour to be gained, duty to be done, dangers to be met, vengeance to be had. Above all, to one who had revered his murdered king there was to be sought the distinction that comes from unwavering integrity in the face of the enemy. So it was that William Edgcumb had taken the command.

The enemy landed at Old Grimsby and took the Abbey by storm. William collected all the men from detached posts, and then counter-attacked so fiercely and for so long that he was on the point of recovering the Abbey. But in the midst of the contest, when success hung in the balance, the building caught fire and was soon ablaze.

William withdrew his men to his last stronghold, the castle named after his king. There he organised his defence and prepared for the end. It was not long in coming.

Admiral Blake brought his ships close by and fired on the castle. On the land the attack was led by Colonel Fleetwood, a stout and tired soldier. The strife was stubborn, but its conclusion inevitable. The fortress was subject to a sudden and desperate assault. When the Parliament's forces were almost in possession, although the day was clearly lost, William refused to surrender. He descended to the magazine, laid a train of powder on the ground and coolly exclaiming 'God save King Charles!' lit the powder.

The earth shook as with an earthquake. There was a breathless lull, then a torrent of flame. The few men remaining on their feet were left full of shock and dismay.

When order had been restored, it was found that though the roof was blown off, the walls were comparatively intact. Hasty repairs were made, 200 Parliamentarians were quartered there and, finally, the dead were gathered and buried in a soldier's grave. However, Edgcumb's body was never found. Under a flag of truce, Sir John Grenville came from St Mary's to demand it for burial. The young cavalier was dear to his general and his comrades and all were anxious to pay their last respects. But their wish could not be granted. All were sure he had perished in the explosion.

Soon Tresco was occupied and a new normality resumed under the stern eye of the Protestants.

King Charles' castle was in ruins, so Fleetwood decided to build a new one at the water's edge where there was already a blockhouse. It was called Cromwell's Castle.

THE LEGEND OF HANGMAN'S ISLAND

Due south of Cromwell's Castle, in the channel between Tresco and Bryher, was an island with tall pyramidal rocks.

'That's Hangman's Island,' Lizzie announced with glee. 'On the summit there's a gibbet.'

After the Civil War had ended, Colonel Fleetwood, who was a widower, brought his daughter Mildred to stay.

She was a pretty young woman, attractive even though she always wore severe Protestant dress with a starched wimple. She had a gaiety not usual in Protestant circles.

But some in the garrison resented her levity and charm and said that no good would come of her presence. Before long others casually accused her of being a scarlet woman.

Then what began as a coarse and unwarranted soldiers' jest ended with a zealot denouncing the girl in church for no reason other than bigotry and malice.

When numbers of the congregation then stood to berate the girl and castigate her father for failing to control her, the colonel reacted with full military authority. The moment more than one of them rose in complaint he could justifiably accuse them of mutiny. A gibbet was erected on the nearby island and the ringleader and five colleagues were sent there.

There they were invited to meditate on the eighth of the Ten Commandments: 'Thou shall not bear false witness' before becoming otherwise preoccupied as they ended their lives dangling and dancing from the gibbet. It's been called Hangman's Island ever since.

Lizzie was altogether cheerful, but Jamie thought how horrible it must be to be hanged and he was glad of a distraction. They walked northward and at Gimble Point they found a deep gulley leading to a tunnel.

'An old adit,' said Lizzie.

PIPER'S HOLE

They walked north-east past overgrown pits and spoil heaps.

'The works go in a line from Gimble Point to Piper's Hole.'

'Piper's Hole? The one that goes to St Mary's?'

'That's what they say,' said Lizzie. 'But I think it's more often used by free traders than errant pipers!'

Soon they were scrambling down the rocks at the north-east corner of the island. The cave entrance was half-blocked with large boulders. Jamie and Lizzie clambered inside. After a few yards they came to a small pool.

'This is as far as the excise men would go!'

Half-buried in the sand, a rope led into the water.

'Help me,' said Lizzie and they both heaved on the rope. The bow of a small dinghy appeared. They tipped the boat on its side so the water would drain and then floated it upright. An oar was tucked under the seat. Then Lizzie expertly sculled across the pool. At its far end was a small gravel beach. Beyond was a tall corridor through the granite. In a few paces they were out of sight of the entrance.

'They keep the goods here,' said Lizzie, 'then, when it's safe, they take them to the Parsonage and hide them in the cellar!'

'They say that long ago it was a tin working, like other caves here. If you know where to look you can see the marks of their picks and drills. But others have been here, too.'

THE LEGEND OF PIPER'S HOLE

After the mutiny and the hangings, Mildred Fleetwood did not dare to seek company. She would wander alone over Tresco, gazing at the distant horizons and wondering what the future might bring.

One evening she went to the north of the island. There she descended a steep ledge of granite and found herself overlooking the cove in which lay Piper's Hole.

Local people told everyone to avoid Piper's Hole as there were the ghosts of those who perished trying to walk between Tresco and St Mary's.

Once a lookout actually saw a grim and threatening figure, ghostly white, emerging from the cave. He was so frightened that he fell in a swoon.

If Mildred knew these tales they did not bother her; perhaps they excited her. But that evening a sudden noise made her turn in alarm.

Nearby stood a young man. His handsome features were pale and wasted; he seemed bowed with pain. His forehead was bound with a scarf, as if to cover a wound. His once fine clothes were torn and stained. Mildred studied him nervously.

'Lady, your features belie your stern clothing, who are you? Why are you in this haunted place? Even bold men avoid Piper's Hole.'

'I am Mildred Fleetwood,' she replied, 'and why should I not come here? But you, who are you, why are you here?'

The young man was silent. He looked at her thoughtfully. His face was gentle, tender even.

'I repeat, who are you, why are you here, where do you live?'

'If you have courage, come and see.'

He held out his hand. After a moment's hesitation, she took it, and he led her towards the cave. There he respectfully asked her to wait. He ran inside, lit a torch, then took her hand and helped her clamber down. In fifty paces they reached a dark pool on which floated a small boat.

'You have come far,' said the youth, 'but you still have a choice. You can turn back or you can continue and find the mystery of Piper's Hole.'

He offered his arm; she took it and climbed into the skiff. A few strokes of the oar sent the vessel across the pool to the sand on the other side. Leaping ashore, he lit another a torch, then helped her from the boat.

In a few paces they reached a vaulted rock-bound room, invisible from the entrance. In one corner was a bed, covered with a soldier's cloak. Weapons lay beside it, many boxes and packages were scattered around and some provisions were in a basket by the head of the couch. All these Mildred took in at a glance. She then looked at her mysterious companion.

Smiling, he said, 'Lady, now you know where I live and you have a right to know the rest. I am William Edgcumbe.'

Mildred started with surprise. Her host was the Royalist leader, supposedly killed defending King Charles' Castle.

He told of his escape from death. He had been flung some way by the explosion that destroyed the castle. But, after lying unconscious he recovered to find himself bruised and weak, but almost without a wound. In the confusion he crawled away unseen and, in the evening, made his way to the Piper's Hole, where he had previously hidden stores. There he was waiting for a chance to escape, living on the hidden rations and food brought by a loyal fisherman. They had acted out the ghostly delusions, which, with the place's bad reputation, had driven away all intruders but for Mildred.

Mildred felt sorry for the young man. When she left there was a tear in her eye. He said he prayed that she would return, and she whispered that she would.

Indeed, she did return, many times. Many were the hours they spent together and many a vow of constancy was given. But, as his eye regained its fire and his step its buoyancy, she grew thoughtful and her cheek was pale.

Then, one evening, he spoke the words she had dreaded. A boat was ready to take him, disguised as a fisherman, past the warships of Parliament and into exile. He asked her to go with him and be his bride.

But Mildred knew she was trusted and loved by her father. Alone in his old age, it would break his heart to part with her. The struggle between love and duty was heart-breaking, but her choice was made. She would stay.

She bade her lover Godspeed, told him to remember her and to expect happier times. After a long embrace they parted: he to exile and she to remain, returning daily to the scene of her vanished happiness and to pray for him who was far away.

Years passed. Ten weary years. They wrote to each other, but with no hope of meeting. But eventually the Protectorate was discredited. In 1660 Charles II returned from exile. He entered London on 29 May, his birthday. That day was made a holiday, known to all as Oak Apple Day.

Then the young lovers' fortunes changed. Honoured by the King, William Edgcumb returned to England. Colonel Fleetwood retired to his estate in Buckinghamshire to live in peace and tranquillity. His old opponent became his son-in-law, and he lived to see grandchildren playing round his hearth. He was more inclined to smile than to shake his head at the romantic adventure of Piper's Hole.

OLIVER'S BATTERY

Back at Old Grimsby Jamie and Lizzie boarded the *Kittiwake*. Soon they were off the southern tip of Tresco. There, on Carn Near, were old ramparts of earth and stone.

'That's what's left of Oliver's Battery,' said Lizzie.

'Oliver?'

'Cromwell, I suppose, or perhaps it was the man that made it. During the Civil War, Admiral Blake built an artillery position here to fire at St Mary's.

'They began on 19 April 1651, building ramparts of earth and rubble on the natural rock.

'On 4 May they set up three culverins, cannons with barrels 12ft long. But it is about 1¾ quarter miles to St Mary's, very long range, and the cannon balls weighed 18lb, so they had to use a high elevation and pack in as many bags of gunpowder as they dared. The fuse was lit. There was an almighty explosion: the culverin had been overcharged and blew apart. Two of the gun crew were killed and others were injured; Blake had a lucky escape. But another culverin was mounted and after three weeks of bombardment the Royalists gave up. They had nowhere left to go.'

Soon they had crossed Appletree Bay, rounded Plumb Island, and moored in New Grimsby, where Anthony was waiting.

BRYHER

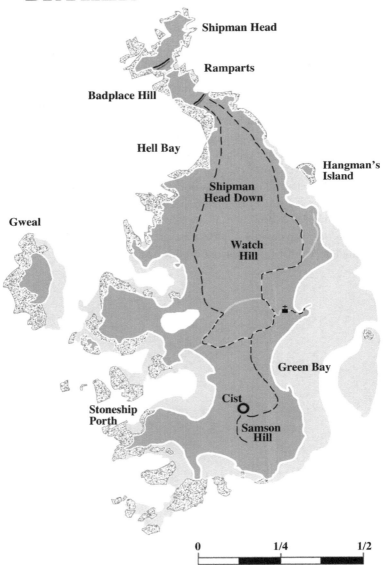

Shipman Head

Ramparts

Badplace Hill

Hell Bay

Hangman's
Island

Shipman
Head Down

Gweal

Watch
Hill

Green Bay

Cist

Stoneship
Porth

Samson
Hill

0   1/4   1/2

8

ETH

BRYHER

Bryher of the five hills, the sword and mirror, the tinners' castle and the bay of hell: final trysting place of a thousand sailors unwillingly wedded to the faithless ocean: here is a 'land beyond', an 'otherworld' that prompted John Trewin to write 'the queen of air and darkness rules in Bryher'.

It was a short sail from New Grimsby to Church Quay on Bryher. The quay extended from a small promontory with a narrow neck that locals called 'the island'. There they were greeted by a figure, venerable and bearded, who took the painter and helped them moor.

THE SEER OF BRYHER

'Welcome, friends. Hicks, Jacob Hicks is my name.'

'Good morning sir,' replied Anthony. Introductions followed.

As they walked inland, other islanders greeted Jacob with deference; clearly, he was well-respected. Their exchanges were intriguing.

'Shall I be fishing today, Jacob?'

'Yes, Sammy, you'll have a fair breeze till sunset and down-tide of Mincarlo will see your net filled.'

'Mornin' Jacob, should I be broadcasting the winter wheat just now?'

'No, William. It's too soon. This fine weather will bring it on too fast, then the frost will have it.'

'Jacob, should I be talking to widow Pender tonight?'

'No, Elias, take her a jug of milk and let her talk to you.'

It seemed that Jacob was the community wise man.

'Bless them all,' said Jacob. 'In my dreams I see their parents, and their grandparents. The angels guard them well, so it's my task to do what I can for those in this lesser heaven until they or I are called to glory.'

Jacob was invested with a unique sanctity. He spoke in a matter-of-fact way, yet retained an air of tranquillity. Like some storytellers, he was a man both of this world and a world beyond. It seemed natural for him to lead them to the church.

THE CHURCH OF ALL SAINTS ON BRYHER

'Praise the Lord,' said Jacob, 'and come inside!'

They crowded into the tiny rectangular building; it was barely eight paces by four.

'Welcome to All Saint's,' said Jacob. 'It's humble enough isn't it. In my dreams I see it with a fine tower, a high roof and a grand chancel. But we are thankful for what we have. Dedicated on 21 November 1742 by Reverend Paul Hathaway, God bless him.

'Before this church was built there was just Tresco Meeting House. If you wanted to be baptised or married or die you had to travel. If the weather was bad you just had to wait.'

At the back of the church, a bell stood on the floor.

'We're going to mount it outside the door when the right timber comes ashore.'

It was a ship's bell. Jamie read out the inscriptions, 'Fregat Shieppet Aurora 1746' and 'Me Fec G. Mayer Holmiae'.

'Swedish,' said Anthony. 'It says "*Frigate Ship Aurora*" and "G. Mayer of Holmia made me". Holmia is near Stockholm.'

'It was 1784,' said Jacob. 'The *Aurora* struck a rock off Land's End, but made it to the Isles of Scilly before sinking near St Helen's. We salvaged the cargo, so they let us keep the bell.'

BRYHER HOLED STONE

They went outside.

'Of course, before the church was made this stone was all they had!'

Beyond the church was a strange standing stone about 4ft high, 2ft wide, and 6in thick. Near the top were two holes, one above the other.

'It's a trysting stone. Young people, engaged to be married, would pass their hands through the holes, and joining them together, there they would plight their troth.'

'In fact, anyone wanting to make a wish would link hands through the stone. Or if you wanted to break a spell you would pass a ring through the holes and say magic words.

'Of course, it's not used now, not officially. Though I do hear that certain promises have been made there and in return certain favours given. It'll probably end up as an ornament in someone's garden.'

THE NEWS ROCK

The walked to the south of Timmy's Hill.

'This is what we call the News Rock,' said Jacob.

'People would gather here when the day's work was done. Gossip, births and deaths, news from faraway places, but nobody much cared about that. The population was under a hundred then, so the news got round fast.'

'That's like the Cornwall Stone,' said Anthony, 'That's a square stone a quarter of a mile from the Godolphin's mansion in Breage. A hundred years ago Sir Sidney Godolphin was a Privy Councillor and First Lord of the Treasury. He knew everything that was going on in the land.

'The gentry of Cornwall would meet at Godolphin House to hear the latest news from London. But their servants would listen to the conversations and then pass the news on to their friends gathered at the Cornwall Stone.

The Seer of Bryher bade them farewell at his cottage door. 'There's lots more to see,' he said. With a friendly wave the travellers continued on their way. After a few minutes they reached the Great Pool, created by centuries of peat digging.

'The only freshwater lake in the Isles of Scilly,' said Lizzie.

Jamie was about to comment when he felt Anthony squeeze his hand tightly and recognised it as a signal to say nothing.

The path continued north past Hell Bay.

'I know about Hell Bay,' said Lizzie. 'It's called that because if there's a strong westerly, ships can't get out and they finish up on the rocks.'

THE CASTLE THAT WASN'T

Fifteen minutes later, Jamie was emphatic. 'That is the worst castle ever! No walls, no towers, no dungeons! Nothing!'

Ahead was the rugged outline of Badplace Hill and Shipman Head, the northernmost headland of Bryher. Anthony had said he knew of a castle there. The youngsters were not impressed.

'The trouble is,' said Anthony, 'all the castles you've seen are less than 500 years old. This one is thousands of years old. In those days they used headlands as castles because the cliffs made walls on three sides. They just had to dig a ditch across the headland then use the earth to make a high bank.

'They would built a wooden palisade on top and for only modest effort had a place that was really hard to attack.'

'I see it!' shouted Lizzie. 'A bank going all the way across. The heather makes it hard to see.'

The youngsters scampered about, then returned to Anthony. 'There are two walls. The first is halfway between the saddle and Badplace Hill. The other is out on Shipman Head, just past a steep gulf. And there are lots of cairns.'

'Ah yes, castles and cairns, boundaries and burials, always on hilltops and cliff edges. The castles defend the land and the old spirits watch over their descendants. It's been that way in Celtic lands for thousands of years. When Ennor was one island this would have been its last outpost. Shipman Head castle was the last watch-tower of Lyonesse.'

They returned past the landing place. The *Kittiwake* was still safe above high water.

Next they came to Veronica Farm. Anthony sniffed the air.

'That'll be a brewhouse for sure.'

Beside the farmhouse was a roughly made single-storey building. Traces of grain on the path confirmed its purpose.

'I expect most people on the out islands mill their corn by hand and brew their own ale. Only on St Mary's are there enough people to justify a windmill.'

THE WARRIOR QUEEN OF ENNOR

They followed the path around the north side of Samson Hill. Below was a myriad of small fields. Lizzie ran to the edge of one of them and scraped away some earth.

'You mustn't tell anyone,' she said. 'It's a secret.'

Just below ground level were rocky slabs. There was a gap between two of them. The space underneath was hollow.

'The Seer showed me: it's a warrior's tomb. You can peer in and see with a match, but you're not allowed to touch.'

'I can see bits of skeleton,' said Jamie. 'A sword, a scabbard, and other things too: an old mirror, a brooch and a ring.'

Anthony looked thoughtful. 'One skeleton, you say?'

'Yes.'

'Swords are usually associated with great warriors and mirrors are usually associated with great ladies. So perhaps this person was both of those.'

'Hooray,' said Lizzie. 'A warrior queen!'

'Some thought that mirrors were magic, to look into another world.'

'So, she could be a magician, too?'

'Who can say? But it's fun to guess,' mused Anthony. 'In those days the islands would still have been linked. She could have been the Queen of Ennor.'

MAIDEN BOWER

They continued south and climbed to the top of Samson Hill.

'Please tell me the view,' asked Anthony.

A tear formed in Jamie's eye as he replied, 'The sun is bright on the sea and rocks cast deep shadows. The waves are in constant motion and sea birds spiral above the spray.'

Lizzie catalogued the landscape, 'There are dozens of little islands and rocks. To the south are Samson, White Island and Mincarlo. West is a line of rocks and little islands stretching out into the ocean: Castle Bryher, Illiswilgig, Seal Rock and Maiden Bower. To the north are Gweal and Scilly Rock.'

'Those names tell us a lot,' said Anthony. 'Gweal means the place of trees. Illiswilgig sounds funny but I bet it was once Enys Weljak, grassy island. Unless they are ironic, those names could date from before the Scillies were inundated. Mincarlo was probably Maen Carlyth, stone of the ray fish.'

'What about Maiden Bower? I thought a bower was a lady's garden, with a couch and climbing plants and hedges.

'Medn dowr: water stone.'

'Amazing names,' said Jamie. 'A story on their own!'

'The important thing is what comes first. Is the place named after the story? Or is the story invented from the place name, like at Tolman Head?

By now the sun was low in the west and a golden pathway of light stretched towards them from the horizon.

'Let's go to Veronica Farm,' said Anthony, 'they might like a tale or two.'

THE CHARMING MOLLY

That evening they continued to talk about the place names. The farmer declared, 'I know a place named from a story, rather than the other way round. It's less than half a mile from here.'

This was his tale:

Captain Samuel Marder was a devout Dorset man. On Thursday, 16 November 1780 he attended evensong at St Mary's, Melcome Regis, then returned to his home at 52 St Thomas Street. There his dining room was on the first floor and, as he ate, he looked out at the Town Bridge over the River Wey. Moored at the Town Quay he could see his brig *Charming Molly*, one of the largest ever built at Weymouth.

Next morning, he rose early and bade his wife Mary a fond farewell. Under his command the *Charming Molly* slipped across to Portland to load stone at King's Pier. The pier was exposed, but thankfully the sea was calm and the tricky business of loading 120 tons of Portland stone went well. Even so, it was more than twelve hours of toil, managed with great care as the stone blocks, each weighing over a ton, could easily injure ship or man. Then, at the end of the day, the crew secured and checked the timber baulks and shuttering needed to keep this heavy cargo safely in position in the centre of the hold. At 8 p.m. they were pleased to leave the quay and set sail on their four-day voyage to Dublin.

The wind was still light and it was slack water at Portland Bill. Even so, the sea was confused, the ship's motion was uncomfortable and the cargo strained against its shuttering. Clear of the headland, when the ship took on a steadier motion, they set topsails; in a gentle southerly wind they headed across Lyme Bay. Marder retired to his bunk, leaving Jenkins the mate in command. With dawn, Start Point was in sight. The wind was now west of south, so they altered course onto west. They set topgallants and soon Start Point was well astern.

By the time they were abeam Plymouth, the wind had veered to south-west and had increased. Even close hauled they were being pushed into St Austell Bay. Off Fowey they tacked, turning the bow of the ship through the eye of the wind. The *Charming Molly* headed south into the open waters of the English Channel.

As they left the land astern the wind increased in strength. It was now force four with gusts to five.

Above them the sky was laced with mares' tails, and in the west the cloud was thickening. Marder nodded approval as Jenkins prudently took in the topsails and topgallants. He reefed the mainsails and the mizzen. They lowered one of the two headsails.

Two hours later, at nightfall, it started to rain gently. They put in a second reef and at ten that evening they tacked again; close hauled, they maintained a course of west-north-west. Marder hoped that they might get a visual sighting of the Lizard to confirm his dead reckoning before heading out into the Southwest Approaches.

As the night passed the wind continued to veer and their close-hauled course came round to north-west. The moon was in its last quarter, but despite the high cloud, they were able to make out the Lizard, and in its lee they tacked again on to west-south-west.

The wind was now force six and gusting higher. The sea state was building all the time and the ship's movement was harsh. Marder cursed quietly; it was always this way with Portland stone, it made the ship's motion abrupt: uncomfortable for the crew, and hard on the rigging.

He thought. The wind was westerly, but he expected it to veer further in the next twelve hours. He considered tacking and sailing between the Seven Stones reef and Land's End. But that would place his ship close to the uncompromising lee shore of North Cornwall. No! It would be safer to continue south-west to gain sea room, then turn to pass west of the Isles of Scilly before heading into the Irish Sea.

Dawn was a watery affair. The rain had increased and the sun seemed unwilling to rise. Throughout the morning the seas continued to build and the rain grew heavier. Then, just after midday, it was time to tack again. The spanker was backed and the helm set to leeward. Slowly, stiffly, the *Charming Molly* turned towards the wind. The seas seemed steeper than ever. Slowly she edged towards the eye of the wind, and there ... there she stopped. Caught in stays, she wallowed helplessly, all the time making sternway.

Marder cursed under his breath, then shouted aloud, 'Ease the spanker,* back the jib!' Slowly, so slowly, the ship turned back towards its original course.

'Stand by to wear ship,' was Marder's command.**

---

*   The spanker is a fore and aft sail set on the mizzen mast.

**   Wearing ship is changing direction by turning the stern through the eye of the wind.

Slowly and uncomfortably the *Charming Molly* turned downwind. Once again, the jib and spanker were used to help turn the ship. After ten minutes they were sheeted in, the mainsails too were set close-hauled, and the heading was north-westerly. The failed tack had cost them half an hour and valuable ground to windward.

As afternoon turned to evening the crew scanned the horizon for the Isles of Scilly. Visibility was poor and they saw nothing. Two hours after sunset, Jenkins thought he might have seen St Agnes light to starboard, but no one was sure.

The seas were now steeper, and Marder guessed that their progress to windward was marginal. He wondered if it would be wise to wear ship again and head out to the south-west.

'Rocks, rocks on the bow!'

The lookout startled Marder from his thoughts. Instinctively he turned starboard, to leeward of the obstruction.

His mind raced. It must be one of Scilly's Western Rocks, but he could not guess which one. Leaving Jenkins at the wheel, he dashed to the chart table. They must have made far more leeway than he had estimated and that failed tack would have cost him several miles. He suspected the rocks must be the Crebinicks or Bishop Rock.

Jenkins skilfully held the ship hard on the wind, but it had veered even further. The best course he could make was north-north-east. Marder knew that the rocks of Scilly must be close to leeward. There was not sea room to wear ship and the steep seas meant that tacking was unlikely to succeed.

Then there was a cry from midships.

'The cargo, the cargo's adrift. The shuttering's broken.'

The constant slamming of the hull had caused 120 tons of Portland stone to break the timbers that bound it.

Normally Marder would have hove-to and repaired the shuttering with the ship relatively stable. But with Scilly to leeward he could not afford to give away any sea room. Nor could he risk his men suffering injury from the great blocks of stone.

He was pondering this when the lookout cried again.

'White water ahead, port and starboard!'

'Strike the mainsails, lower the anchor,' cried Marder.

The *Charming Molly* lurched to port as he spun the wheel to turn the ship to windward. But after only a few degrees' alteration of heading she stopped turning, the steep seas crashing against the bow.

Then there was a jarring thump as she struck. A wave lifted her, then she thumped again. Again and again the cruel litany was repeated. The anchor was released, but it dragged immediately.

'Water, water in the hold.'

Marder knew the ship was doomed. In the darkness he perceived land to the south-east, now only yards away.

'Everyone amidships,' he ordered.

The stern struck; the ship spun round beam on to the waves. Then the bow too impacted the rock ledges of Bryher. The *Charming Molly* listed at a crazy angle. Marder heard the rumble of Portland stone and the cracking of timbers.

On the shore he saw figures, close, yet a world away.

'The mainsheet, throw it to leeward.'

Jenkins paid out the mainsheet over the leeward rail, and wind and wave carried it ashore.

'Right, take the heaving line, tie it round young Jimmy's waist as a safety line. Jimmy, over you go, follow the mainsheet. When you're safe untie yourself.'

'Aye, Capn!'

Jimmy, the youngest crew member, plunged into the water holding the mainsheet. Jenkins paid out the heaving line. After 30 yards the lad reached the arms of rescuers in shallow water.

The heaving line was untied and pulled back on board. One by one all twelve of the crew made their way to safety. Finally, alone on the ship, with a heavy heart Marder said, 'Goodbye old girl,' then himself plunged into the icy water.

The waves tore at him, the backwash sucked him towards the sea, but he gripped the mainsheet with all his might. After thirty seconds of struggle his feet touched bottom. Moments later, strong hands grasped him and pulled him ashore.

To this day the little cove where the *Charming Molly* came ashore is called Stoneship Porth. But where the valuable cargo of Portland stone cargo went, no one can tell.

CROSSING THE RED SEA

Next morning Anthony returned to Tresco with the farmer. Jamie and Lizzie played on the silver sand before returning to the quay. But there they found not one but two boats. By the slip was the *Kittiwake*. Beside it was Godolphin's tender.

'Time for you to come with us.'

Behind them stood the Penzance constable and his runner. The children were trapped on the promontory.

Lizzie ran to the *Kittiwake*. The corks were missing from the drain holes in the stern.

In the constable's hand were the corks. Smiling, he tossed them far into the sea.

'You're going nowhere and this young fellow's coming with us. My master will be pleased to hear that I've caught the lad that caused him so much trouble with the press gang.'

In a trice Lizzie reached into Godolphin's tender, pulled out the bung and threw it into the tide.

The constable was horrified. 'What did you do that for? Now we're all stuck. I'll make you pay for that.'

He lunged at Lizzie but she nimbly dodged aside.

'Harry, you go and get help, I'll keep an eye on these two. At least they can't run away. They'll cool off in a minute.'

The constable sat down on the neck of land between the promontory and the rest of the island. It did seem that they could not escape. Lizzie looked towards Tresco. In the channel, rocks and sand were still visible. A couple of seals swam nearby, looking inquisitively at the shore.

'That's half-tide bar,' she whispered. 'I've got an idea.'

She turned to her would-be captor. 'As we are stuck, why don't I tell you a story?'

The constable lay on the grass, 'It'll pass the time.'

'How about a Bible story? Moses crossing the Red Sea?'

'Haven't you got anything better than that?'

'All right,' said Lizzie, and the story began.

THE BEAR'S REVENGE

'Not very long ago, there was a sailing ship coming to England from foreign parts. Among the cargo was a dancing bear in a wooden cage on the deck. During the voyage the nastier members of the crew cruelly taunted this bear. They poked it with sticks and teased it to make it perform for them. The bear was unhappy and there was no doubt that it knew just who was persecuting it. But the bear was safely locked in its cage, which was lashed to the deck of the ship.

'Anyway, near the end of the voyage the ship encountered the most terrible weather and eventually was driven onto the rocks west of Scilly. Not far from here actually. The waves began breaking the hull and it seemed the crew would all be drowned, so they lowered their longboat into the sea and began rowing for the shore.

'However, not only were the waves wild enough to break the ship's hull, they were wild enough to break apart the bear's cage. At this point the bear realised there was nothing between it and those that had tormented it during the voyage. So, bent on revenge, the bear jumped into the sea and started swimming after the longboat.

'Now the angry bear was better at swimming than the frightened sailors were at rowing. To their horror the bear caught up with the longboat. But the boat was already full. One more body on board would certainly sink it.

'Alas, the sailors did not have the sense to keep the bear at bay with their oars. The bear put one paw on the stern, then another. It began to climb in over the transom of the boat. With the extra weight, the stern dipped, the water poured in and the boat and its crew went straight to the bottom of the ocean.

'So it was that the bear got its revenge.

'But no one knows what happened to the bear. Some say he is still there, swimming from island to island, looking for the something, or someone, to eat.'

The constable laughed. Then suddenly he looked up. With the last word of the tale Jamie and Lizzie had sprinted for the water's edge and were now were splashing across the channel towards Tresco.

'Low water springs,' whispered Lizzie to Jamie, 'It's the only time it's possible.'

'Come back!' said the constable. 'You'll drown.'

'We'll take the chance.'

The constable plunged into the sea after them. Already the tide had turned. The water was getting deeper by the minute.

Lizzie did not head directly across but first led Jamie south, then south-east. The constable cut the corner and at first it looked as if he was catching up. But though the water was up to the children's knees, the constable was soon floundering in ever deeper water.

'Time to enlist some help,' said Lizzie. She turned to the constable. 'Watch out for the bear!' she shouted.

By chance a friendly seal surfaced about 10ft from the constable and barked at him.

The constable screamed, lost his footing and disappeared under the rising water. Then, spluttering and splashing, he swam towards the rocky island in the middle of the channel.

'Don't worry,' shouted Lizzie, 'We'll send you two barley loaves and a pitcher of water!'

'What does that mean?' asked Jamie.

Lizzie shouted, 'In the old days they left criminals on a rock with bread and a pitcher till they were drowned by the tide!'

There was a wail from the midst of the channel.

'That rock's always above water,' whispered Lizzie. 'But I don't think we'll tell him that!'

Lizzie and Jamie turned north-east towards Plumb Beach. Soon they were scrambling ashore.

WALKING ON WATER

'How?' asked Anthony. 'No one saw your sail.'

'We walked,' said Jamie.

'On the water? Is your name St Peter?'

Lizzie said that while Peter may have been the name of the constable it was unlikely he would ever become a saint.

'In the time of Henry VIII, Tresco, Bryher and Samson were joined together. You can still sometimes walk between them and from St Martin's you can still get to White Island, Little Ganilly and Great Arthur. But you have to be very careful and cross quickly at low water spring tides. Where the channels are narrowest they are deepest so you have to go with someone who knows the way.'

'But it's not spring, it's autumn.'

'Spring tides are those with the biggest rise and fall; they happen twice a month.

'I wonder what it was like in the old days,' asked Jamie.

'Legend says there was a Roman Road from St Mary's to Tresco. The Seer of Bryher told me his dad knew of people walking between St Mary's and the off-islands, but that was more than a hundred years ago. Now it's far too deep, but you can still work out the route. From Bar Point on St Mary's they followed Crow Bar north-north-west until abeam Guther's Island and then turned right or left for St Martin's or Tresco.'

Then Lizzie got corks from the inn at New Grimsby and a friendly boatman took her to Bryher to fetch the *Kittiwake*.

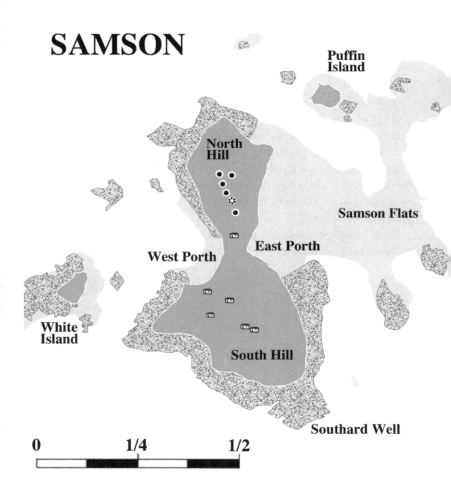

SAMSON

Puffin
Island

North
Hill

Samson Flats

West Porth

East Porth

White
Island

South Hill

Southard Well

0   1/4   1/2

9

NAW

SAMSON

Gazing across Samson, you gaze into the past. Half close your eyes, let the breeze touch your cheek and the voices return, the fields are fertile and children play in the bracken. Open your eyes and they fly as a dream in the dawn.

In the first light of dawn they sailed to Samson.

'Anthony?' asked Lizzie. 'The hills on Samson, North Hill and South Hill. The Seer said they were *devron*. What's that?'

'It's half-remembered Cornish, Dew vron: two breasts. Some people say it's what the hills look like.'

They went ashore at East Porth, the beach between the hills, and hid the little boat in the bracken.

SAINT SAMSON

'I know about Samson from the Bible,' said Lizzie. 'He was a strong man who told riddles. He killed a lion with his bare hands and beat a whole army with the jawbone of an ass.'

'Woah!' said Anthony. 'What you have said is fine, but that's the wrong Samson. The Samson of this island was a saint who was born in South Wales in about the year 485. He was a pupil of Saint Illtud.*

'Then he came to Cornwall: St Kew and Golant. Tradition says that he came here, too. Finally he went to Dol in Brittany, where he was made a bishop.'

THE PILOT GIG

Also hidden in the bracken nearby was a slender rowing boat.

'It's a pilot gig,' said Lizzie. 'Pilots are the best sailors; they guide ships into port. It's such an important job that they are appointed by the twelve men of Scilly.'**

'How do they know when they are needed?' asked Jamie.

'Ships wanting a pilot show the flag "G"; blue and yellow stripes. There are lookouts on all the islands. The gigs row the pilots out. The first one to reach the ship gets the job, so the fastest gigs with best rowers are the richest.'

The graceful craft was about 26ft long and had four oars.*** The maker's name was on the stern: Wm. Peters, St Mawes.

'Why don't they just have more oars?' asked Jamie.

'They are not allowed more oars,' said Lizzie. 'If they had five they would go round in circles, and if they had six they could outrun the revenue cutters.'

'Ah yes,' said Anthony, 'like the *Happy Go Lucky*.'

Lizzie looked embarrassed. 'Yes, they are used for other things. In summer they even go to Brittany for trading.'

'Also, the gigs are often used to rescue people. But it's very dangerous. Not long ago seven pilots were drowned trying to rescue sailors from the Western Rocks. Six widows and twenty-seven children

---

*   Pronounced ith-tid.

**   From 1808 they were licensed by Trinity House.

***   From 1829 six oars were allowed.

were left. They had a collection; it raised just £40. Two more drowned trying to salvage the *Fortune*. That was a pretty poor fortune, too.'

SCADS AND TATERS

As Lizzie finished, Jamie looked up. As if from nowhere children had silently appeared. Two, then four, eventually twenty-four of them. Their clothes were ragged and they were painfully thin. Silently they held out their hands.

'What have we got?' asked Jamie.

Between them they had half a loaf of bread, three pieces of cheese, an onion and an oatcake.

Silently the children wolfed down the food, then vanished into the bracken of South Hill. A pale woman appeared.

'Thank you,' she said, 'but what do you want? We have nothing here. Just a few potatoes and limpets on the rocks.'

'We tell stories,' said Jamie.

'Of course you do. Who are you hiding from?'

'The constable from Penzance.'

'He was here two days ago. What did you steal?'

'Nothing.'

'Of course … There's nothing to steal here.'

'There are six families here?' asked Anthony.

'Thirty-six souls. Woodcocks and Webbers. How we survive I don't know. There's little wrecking and the free-trading is getting worse every year. Soon all the off-islands will be starving. They say that years ago there were fertile fields right across to Tresco, but there's none now.'

She nodded to the east. Where they had landed were now acres of sand and mud. The field walls ran straight from the land, across the flats and under the water.

'The sea took it all.'

'Two of our lads are boatmen. Two others fish: conger in the day and scad at sunset. Everyone else works on the land or gathers shellfish. You know what they say don't you?

Scads and 'taters, scads and 'taters,
Scads, and 'taters, and conger,
And those who can't eat scads and 'taters
Oh, they must die of hunger.

'It's true, even the last bit. That's why Scillonian proverbs are all about food and fish. Things like "There is always a feast or a fast in Scilly" and "Oh! the Scillonians live on fish and 'taties every day, and conger pie for Sundays".

'I don't know how much longer we'll stay. It's no place for the kids. Even the dogs wouldn't stay here.'

Jamie looked inquisitive.

'Last week every dog on the island, all fourteen of them, ran into the sea together and were drowned. Like rats leaving a sinking ship. I think it's a message for us.'

'Is there a place we could shelter for the night?'

'You can sleep on our floor. It's the house on the right.'

'Thank you.'

As the woman returned to her cottage, Jamie clutched Anthony's hand. 'What shall we do?' he said.

'I think we should stay one night, then we see if we can return to St Mary's. We shouldn't impose on these people.'

Feeling rather downcast, they clambered on to North Hill. There was a stone circle and several cairns and cists.

'Like Bryher, this was the borderland: the place of the watcher, the place of the ancestors. And I suspect that soon all that will be left here will be its stories.'

TRISTAN AND ISEULT

Anthony continued, 'Legend has it that Samson is the place where Tristan of Cornwall fought the Irish giant Morold.'

'Who won?'

'Let me start at the beginning. Tristan was a squire to Mark, the King of Cornwall. In those days Irish pirates used to raid Cornwall and demand tribute. They would take away young men and women to be slaves. No one dared fight them because the Irish champion, Morold, was a giant man who had never been defeated. But one day when the Irish attacked, Tristan took up Morold's challenge. The battle was long and hard. Morold just touched Tristan with his sword.

"It's nothing," said Tristan, "Just a scratch."

'Morold laughed, "But the tip of my sword was dipped in poison. No one in the world can cure it except my sister, the Queen of Ireland, and she will never help you."

'Morold was still laughing when Tristan buried his sword in his skull and killed him. But a fragment of the blade stuck in Morold's head and a notch was missing from Tristan's sword.

'So, Tristan disguised himself as a minstrel. He sailed to Ireland, where he pretended he had been bitten by a snake. There the queen healed him and he was nursed back to health by her daughter, who was called Iseult. She was very beautiful and when Tristan got home he wrote a poem describing her beauty. King Mark read the poem and then sent Tristan to Ireland to ask the queen if her daughter would marry the King of Cornwall. She agreed.

'But on the voyage back to Cornwall Iseult noticed Tristan's sword had a fragment missing from the blade and realised he must be the man who had killed her uncle Morold.

'Iseult wanted to avenge her uncle, so she put some poison in two glasses of wine and she and Tristan both drank it.'

'That's awful,' said Jamie.

'Aha!' smiled Anthony. 'But the Queen of Ireland had made Iseult's maid, Branwen, promise to let no harm come to Iseult. When she saw Iseult was about to drink the poison she swapped the bottle with another one, so they were saved.'

'That was lucky!'

'Maybe. The new bottle contained a love potion so they both fell in love. But Iseult was supposed to be marrying Mark.'

'What happened next?'

'Well,' said Anthony, 'this story has two possible endings, a sad one

or a happy one. Which one do you want?'

Lizzie answered, 'This is a sad place, let's have the happy ending.'

'Neither Mark nor Tristan would agree to let the other marry Iseult. So they asked King Arthur to decide.

'Arthur decided that Iseult should be shared and spend six months of the year with one man and six with the other!'

'That's not right!' protested Lizzie.

'I agree,' said Anthony, 'but it is only a story.

'Arthur said that one man should have Iseult in the summer and the other should have her in the winter. Mark was a king so he was allowed to decide first. Mark wanted Iseult to keep him warm in the long nights of winter so he declared, "Iseult will be my queen when the leaves fall from the trees."

'But then Tristan produced a sprig of holly that, of course, has green leaves all the year round. So he and Iseult were married after all and lived happily ever after.'

'There is a suggestion,' Anthony continued, 'that Saint Samson knew the real Tristan. Their dates could have been similar. Samson and his island are never far from this story.'

HMS *COLOSSUS*

'When I was little,' said Lizzie, 'there was a wreck just south-east of Samson, HMS *Colossus*.'

'I heard of it,' said Anthony.

'Last year they came looking for guns. The officer told us the story.'

HMS *Colossus* was a 74-gun ship of the line that fought at the battles of the Nile and Cape St Vincent. In 1798, under Captain George Murray, she was in Naples.

The British envoy in Naples was the antiquarian Sir William Hamilton. His wife, Lady Emma, was the young actress who was Nelson's mistress. In 1772 Hamilton's first collection of Greek and Roman antiquities had helped to found the British Museum. By 1796 he had gathered another collection, even finer than the first. But in 1798 Naples was threatened by Napoleon. Sir William and Lady Emma fled the city.

HMS *Colossus* was ordered back to England. Sir William's priceless antiquities were loaded on board. Before departing, Murray transferred three guns and a bower anchor to Admiral Nelson's flagship, HMS *Vanguard*, which was to remain in the war zone. Then *Colossus* began her journey home …

It was 7 December. Captain Murray gritted his teeth; a south-easterly gale was cruel! It would test both ship and crew after the weary thirty-day voyage from Naples. Sheltering in the Isles of Scilly was the prudent course of action.

Before long they were anchored in the lee of the Garrison. The best bower anchor was lowered and all cable deployed, all the chain in the locker.* Murray regretted having given one of his anchors to the *Vanguard*, but the best bower held. For three days the storm increased. Murray ordered the topgallant masts to be lowered to reduce windage. Second and third anchors were prepared.

At four in the afternoon of 10 December there was a sound like a gunshot. The ship's motion abruptly changed. Although brand new, the cable had parted and *Colossus* was drifting downwind towards Samson.

'Lower the number two bower!'

The spare bower anchor was let go. It bit, the chain pulled tight, then under strain it jerked free.

'Pilot,' called Murray, 'let's put to sea, ride out the storm.'

'It's nearly dark,' was the reply. 'We'll never make it to open water.'

'The sheet anchor, lower the sheet anchor,' ordered the captain. 'Strike the yards and topmasts.'

The sheet anchor was their last hope. The *Colossus* was dragging downwind at half a knot. Samson was a mile away. In two hours they would be aground. The anchor chains jerked and tugged. The ship shuddered under the strain.

Closer and closer came the island. Neither anchor would set. Then at about half-past five, the bower anchor bit. As the ship veered they took the strain on the sheet anchor, hoping the *Colossus* could ride between the two. But even as they did so, the ship grated to a halt on the rock ledge of Southard Well, three cables south-east of Samson.

---

*   A bower anchor is a ship's main anchor, mounted at the bow.

In the bowels of the ship the pumping gangs worked with all their might. The ship was only just touching. At the top of the flood they might be able to haul her free.

Suddenly there was a pitiful cry. Quartermaster King had fallen overboard. The ship had lurched as he was sounding the lead. They threw ropes in the hope he might grasp one, but in vain: he vanished forever in the darkness.

About 8 o'clock the wind veered to the south and the ship swung round. The dead man's soundings gave some hope. Men were set to the capstans; slowly, very slowly both cables were taken in.

Suddenly there was a huge crash as the *Colossus* struck again. The ship shuddered, timbers splintered, the rigging groaned.

'The water is gaining on the pumps!' came the cry. Men were sent to bale with half-tubs and buckets.

The wind strength increased; so did the water level. Then at midnight there was another mighty shock.

'The rudder's gone!'

The pounding had knocked it clean off its pintles. The water level now made pumping impossible.

Distress flares were lit, but with no hope of help until dawn.

A chill came over Murray. The next ebb could push the ship to the south into deeper water; the next flood could submerge the ship. In that case it would be all able men into the rigging until rescue came.

By three in the morning the water was up to the gun ports on the upper deck. Murray ordered his crew to the quarter deck and poop. Almost awash, the ship rolled violently, striking the rocks again and again.

Then, wonder of wonders, with the dawn came a fleet of small boats rowing out from St Mary's.

Through the storm the young men of Scilly came to the rescue. Murray directed the sick and invalids into the first boat, then division by division the rest embarked. By three in the afternoon Murray saw the last man out of the ship.

Another hour and all would surely have been lost, as the storm increased yet more and no small craft could have survived. As it was, some of them could not make headway and were forced to land on

Bryher. But the rest returned to St Mary's. The crew outnumbered the inhabitants of Hugh Town, but each household took a share of the men and tended them as best they could.

By daylight next morning the ship was on her beam ends; she had toppled over in the night. So ended that last voyage of the *Colossus*. Hamilton's priceless collection of antiquities was lost forever, but one bower anchor was safe with Nelson on HMS *Vanguard*.

As usual following a loss, a court martial was convened, at which George Murray was cleared of any blame. After a distinguished career he retired as a vice-admiral.

'Did they find any of the guns?' asked Anthony.

'Yes, they had a water glass to look at the sea bed.'

'I never heard of such a thing. What was it like?'

'Like a little barrel with a glass bottom. You just put it in the water and look down. You can see fishes and everything!'

They chatted for a while, then Lizzie went to explore the rocks at the north end of the island. Jamie helped Anthony down to the cottage where they were to spend the night. They were greeted by the pale-faced lady.

'Elizabeth Webber. There's no food for you I'm afraid.'

'Anthony James, and this is my lad Jamie. We understand.'

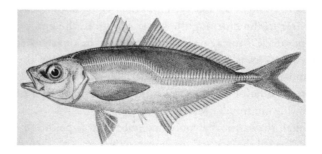

They had never seen such a dwelling. There were two small rooms. The larger had an open range, but the only furniture was two large stones with grass hassocks for seats and two planks for a table. Children seemed to be everywhere.

Just then the door burst open. The children crouched, wide-eyed with fear.

'Supper!' In came Lizzie. In her hand were six small fish.

Spontaneously, everyone cheered.

That evening they told stories to the children. Then Elizabeth went up a ladder to a half-loft. Everyone else lay wrapped in blankets on dry bracken on the floor, the children cuddling for warmth till they fell asleep to the sound of the sea.

In the morning the children lined up on the beach and silently waved as they set sail.

'You'll not be back,' said Elizabeth. 'No one ever comes back.'

They headed towards St Mary's. But after only a few minutes' sailing the distinctive outline of Godolphin's ketch was visible, still alongside the quay.

'In that case,' said Lizzie, 'there's only one thing to do, we must sail on to St Agnes.'

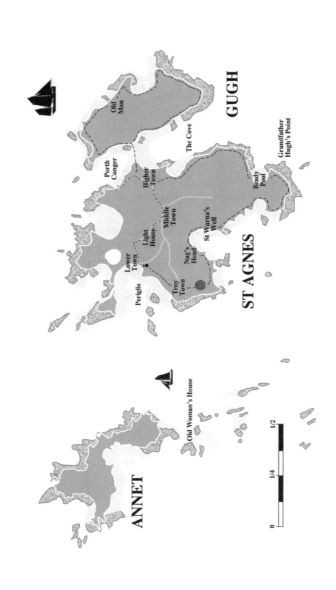

ANNET

Old Woman's House

0   1/4   1/2

PORTH
CONGER

Old
Man

GUGH

The Cove

Higher
Town

Light
House

Middle
Town

Lower
Town

St Warna's
Well

Periglis

Beady
Pool

Troy
Town

Nag's
Head

Grandfather
Hugh's Point

ST AGNES

10

DEG

ST AGNES AND THE WESTERN ROCKS

By night, south-west of St Agnes, every island, every rock, has its splash of reflected light. Through the moving prism of the waves, Annet and the Western Rocks become the moon and stars of the endless sea.

The wind was from the north-east and the voyage to St Agnes was swift. Soon they entered Porth Conger, the inlet between St Agnes and Gugh. As they swung alongside the quay, Jamie hopped ashore. Lizzie looked out to sea. The swell had been building all morning and in the Porth it was steep.

'We must get her above the high-water mark,' she shouted.

At the top of the slipway were some wooden rollers and with their aid they started to push the little boat clear of the water, but the slipway was steep and progress was slow.

'Let me help you.' A tall sailor from a nearby cottage helped push the boat beyond the reach of the threatening waves.

'Hicks, Joseph Hicks,' the sailor introduced himself. 'Welcome to Higher Town. Storytellers eh? Come with me. You need to speak to my cousin Badger up in Middle Town. Abraham Hicks is his real name. He is a farmer by trade but his parlour is, er, a place where people gather.'

It was a short walk to Middle Town. Joseph knocked on a door and cried out, 'Hey Badger, I've got some storytellers here.'

'Stories?' answered Abraham. 'Are you friends of that Reverend Whitworth?'

'No,' said Anthony with quiet authority. 'Mr Whitfield is not a friend of ours.'

'Ah, you're welcome, please step inside.'

Badger, suddenly genial, was a mine of information. His wife Susan was a mine of hospitality.

THE NAME OF THE ISLAND

'We don't get many visitors,' he said. 'Do you know how St Agnes got its name?'

'No,' replied Anthony.

'Neither does anybody else!' said Badger. 'Originally it was just Agnes, or something like it. Some say the name is Viking: Hagenes.'*

Anthony chipped in, 'The Norwegian "hage" means garden, and in medieval times there was a field here belonging to the monks of Tresco. "Nes" means headland. So perhaps the Vikings came raiding and found a garden here.'

Badger grinned mischievously, 'Then after the Reformation someone put the "saint" there to make it like the other islands. Trying to make us look holy!'

'Of course, Agnes is the patron saint of gardeners.'

Badger smiled, 'I like the Viking idea best.'

'So do I,' laughed Anthony.

'Here, did you know I'm famous? A relative of mine, Lt Zachary Hicks, was second in command of Captain Cook's ship the *Endeavour*. On 19 April 1770 he was the first on that ship to sight Australia. They call the place Point Hicks.'

'Are you sure he was a relative of yours?'

'Of course!' Hicks rolled his eyes. 'But let me tell you a proper story. There are older tales *about* the islands. But this is one of the oldest *from* the islands.'

---

*   Noted in the year 1194.

THE GREAT AGNES TRAGEDY

'Years ago, before the Reformation, there were just five families on Agnes. Two of the youngsters fell in love and agreed to be married. In those days the only church was on St Mary's, so on the appointed day five boats sailed across for the ceremony. But when the wedding was over, as they sailed back, a great storm blew up. All five boats were overwhelmed and every man, woman and child on board was drowned. It was practically the whole population of the island. Never, before or since, has such a calamity descended on a community.

'The place was deserted for a generation or more.

'The tale was told to the traveller Leyland in about 1540, so it shows what a huge impact it must have had. The sea is a cruel mistress.'

'Sad indeed,' said Anthony, 'but it tells us there was then a church on St Mary's but none on St Agnes.'

FACT AND FICTION

'Why did you ask if we were friends of Mr Whitfield?' enquired Anthony.

Badger bolted the door.

'Whitfield and his friend Mr Woodley are from far away; they don't know our customs or folklore. But see what they have written!

'They call Warna the saint of shipwrecks and link her to all manner of evil-doing. They write of prayers for wrecks, false lanterns on cows' horns. But it's all fiction.

'Out there are the most dangerous rocks in the world. The Receiver of Wreck is in Plymouth; the Coroner is in Penzance. Starving islanders can't ignore flotsam and jetsam that for them may be the difference between life and death.

'Wrecks occur many times a year and in the worst weather. Our men risk their lives to try and rescue those poor sailors. But some of what those writers have said is just cruel. An example is Whitfield's version of the St Agnes tragedy.'

THE LEGEND OF THE AGNES TRAGEDY

Long ago St Agnes had just five poor families. The Reformation had then replaced the old faith with stern Protestantism. But the islanders still bowed before the altar of St Warna. They prayed and threw pins into her well, for they believed she guided shipwrecks to their island. And many wrecks there were, so the islanders grew wealthy, convinced of the role of their malign saint.

Missionaries tried to reform the islanders, but they stoned them and drove them away. People foretold an evil end, but the people of St Agnes ignored every warning.

One day a vessel approached St Agnes on a dangerous heading. The islanders knelt before the shrine of Warna, vowed their offerings, then ran to the shore.

The ship passed Annet, but then she struck a rock and broke asunder. All on board were hurled into the sea but the islanders ignored their cries and went on seizing what they could.

But then a mass of timbers was washed to the shore. Three or four times it was brought in by the waves and then sucked out by the backwash. Then above the storm came a cry. It came from the broken wood, tossed between sea and land.

On it were two figures. A white-haired old priest was lashed to a plank. In his arms was a beautiful child.

The old minister looked to those on shore, but the wreckers did nothing to help. Every wave weakened the old man. Soon his eyes glazed and he breathed no more. Even in death he clung to the child, but its cries too became feeble and it died.

That night the leader of the wreckers had a terrifying vision.

Beside his bed stood two figures. One was the priest drowned that day, no longer pleading for help but solemn and majestic.

The other figure was St Warna.

Warna raised her arm, saying, 'Priest, why do you come to trouble us? These are my children, do not harm them.'

'You are a false teacher,' said he. 'You and your children shall soon be no more. They that live by the wreck shall die by the wreck. Soon this isle of sin shall be desolate. They who now pollute it shall die the death they have given to others; your shrine will vanish from the face of the earth.'

Then there was silence; the ghostly figures melted away.

The impression made by this vision did not last. Next day the hardened sinner went about his plunder as usual. When he told others of the vision, they laughed. The girl to whom he was engaged joked that her lover needed something else to distract him at night. He went on gathering flotsam and preparing for his wedding, soon to take place at St Mary's.

The morning of the wedding arrived. It was dark and lowering. The channel between Gugh and St Mary's had a heavy swell and the wind blew in squalls. After a stormy passage the five families reached Old Town. Uncomfortably they entered the church. After the wedding the clerk rebuked them for their evil ways. They replied with profanities and mockery. There was nearly a fight between them.

Then the wedding party set out for home. By then the wind had increased to a gale and from a gale to a tempest. Just beyond the Pulpit rock a great sea broke over them, smashing every boat asunder. Not one person escaped. The wreckage, as if directed by an avenging Providence, was found later in St Warna's bay. So the priest's prophecy came true. St Agnes was deserted; none visited the shrine of St Warna.

Later new settlers came to the island. They had never heard of Warna. They did not clear her well on the day after Twelfth Day. It became choked and her name lived only in legend. All that remains are the old stories.

THE SEA LILY

Another example is Woodley's 'St Warna's Well':

> Pin in the well, pin in the well,
> Moonlight never your secret tell,
> Warna ring your silver bell,
> Bring me a wreck by morning.

Romantic isn't it! In Woodley's tale, Arthur and Ursula Treguile heart-lessly plunder the wreck of a ship called the *Sea Lily*. But the truth was quite different.

The *Zeelelye* was a Dutch East Indiaman. In 1795, she was sailing home to Amsterdam. Her cargo included more than 2 million pieces of Ching Dynasty porcelain valued at 716,139 Dutch guilders, about £140,000. But she was captured by a British naval squadron. The *London Chronicle* reported that en route to London under a prize crew, on Sunday, 20 September about 3 o'clock, she was 'by the violence of the winds, cast upon rocks, bulged (sic) and lost'. She struck the Wee, a rock 3 miles west of St Agnes. Twenty-four men were lost, and forty-five were saved, largely thanks to the islanders.

The valuable cargo meant the wreck was widely debated. *The Times* reported: 'The accident is said to have been wholly occasioned by the obstinacy of the person on board having the command, and who was in time, by those on board, apprised of the immediate danger, told what the light was, and that the land breakers were running a-head.'

The wreck was the fault of the prize master. There is no evidence that any islander acted improperly.

Badger looked grim, 'Woodley had once been a journalist. He surely knew the newspaper reports and the attribution of blame, but instead he chose to malign our people.'

THE NAME OF CRUELTY

'Whitfield also wrote that a sailor, left clinging to a rock, offered a crew from St Agnes a large sum of gold as the price of his rescue, but they took his money and left him to die.'

'Tell me,' said Badger. 'How could they get the money without being in reach of its owner?'

'Here's another. A friend, whose craft had capsized, managed to swim to a point in the waves. His companions came near, and threw out their grapnel, to swing round to him. But the current was strong, the gale fierce, and there seemed a good chance of losing their grapnel, so they hauled it up and pulled away, and the poor fellow was drowned. The boatmen were all from one family and for this act, which was too much even for Agnes, they got a surname, indicating cruelty, that their descendants bear to this day.'

Badger drained his tankard, 'At Periglis are the graves of our men who have died trying to save sailors from the sea. Names like Hicks, Legg, Humphries and Mortimer. They don't suggest cruelty to me. But think about Woodley's fictitious name "Treguile". Perhaps that's what Whitfield is referring to. He made it all up. What do you think?'

Anthony replied, 'Folk tales are usually hallowed by antiquity and most have a grain of truth or wisdom, sometimes more than a grain. But the important thing is that a folk tale has been told and retold, shaped by the life experience of generations of storytellers. That's what gives a folk tale authenticity, what academics call cultural integrity. Written fiction can look similar, but it lacks that quality and it's wrong to imply that it's been through such a process.'

As they stood to leave, Badger was encouraging.

'You must see the light, and the church, then visit Troy Town. 'Tis fine, almost a city. You might see Uncle Tom down there. Then you can have a drink at the Nag's Head and visit St Warna's Well. Oh, and watch out for the lobster man!'

With these instructions echoing in their ears they set off.

ST AGNES LIGHT

At the top of the island, they paused at the lighthouse.

'What's it like, Jamie?' asked Anthony.

'It's a circular white tower about 60ft high. There are windows at the top ...'

A new voice took up the tale: '... and inside are oil lamps made of copper with revolving reflectors driven by clockwork.' The lighthouse keeper had emerged from his tower.

'Built for the Master Wardens and Assistants of the Guild Fraternity or Brotherhood of the most glorious and undivided Trinity and of St Clement in the Parish of Deptford Strond in the County of Kent, otherwise known as Trinity House, a private corporation governed under a Royal Charter on behalf of His Majesty's Government!'

There was a stunned silence. No reasonable conversation could follow such an outburst.

'Why?' asked Lizzie, ever practical.

'In the seventeenth century the number of shipwrecks was so bad that in 1680 Trinity House began a survey of the coasts of England. They found that many charts were wrong; the Isles of Scilly were plotted 10 miles north of their true position.

'Trinity House was also allowed to build lighthouses. Because the Western Rocks are so dangerous, St Agnes was one of the first. Above the doorway is the inscription 'Erected by Capt. Hugh Till and Capt. Symon Bayly 1680'. That was Eighteen years before Henry Winstanley built his lighthouse on the Eddystone Rocks south of Plymouth.

'Poor Winstanley and his light vanished for ever in the great storm of 27 November 1703. But our light is still standing.

'There were two protests against the building of St Agnes light. The first was from the Isle of Wight, complaining that they would lose revenue from harbour dues and victualling as shipping would prefer to use the Isles of Scilly. The second was from the Governor of Scilly complaining that he would lose money from wrecks! Would you like to come and look?' Anthony declined, but Jamie and Lizzie followed the keeper up the stairs. At the top the view was magnificent.

'At first the light came from a coal fire burning in a big open basket called a chauffer. One keeper's wife is said to have pushed her husband into it because he was too free with the local lasses! It was replaced by oil lamps in 1790. My job is to trim the lamps, keep the oil topped up and wind up the clockwork. The clockwork turns the reflectors three times a minute, so that's how often ships see the light flash.'*

SAVED AND LOST

In 1796 the famous Cornish seaman Sir Charles Penrose was the captain of HMS *Cleopatra*, a 32-gun frigate. He was sailing from Halifax, Nova Scotia, for duties in the English Channel. The voyage home was tempestuous and navigation all but impossible. One night, after weeks at sea, by dead reckoning Penrose thought he was entering the Channel. The wind was aft and the *Cleopatra* was making swift progress. Although the captain was unwell, he was on deck and to starboard he spotted a light. He knew it could only be St Agnes lighthouse. It meant that the *Cleopatra* was between the Isles of Scilly and the cliffs of Land's End.

---

* Later the rate was changed to once per minute.

Straight away, Captain Penrose altered course to the south. But no sooner had he done this when he saw, close astern in the dark night, a wave breaking under the bow of a large ship, on the very same course that he had been steering only minutes before.

Captain Penrose waved, shouted through the megaphone, threw up lights and fired guns to try and attract the ship's attention, but all to no avail. The mystery ship vanished into the night, its course unchanged.

That ship was never seen again. Wreckage was found the next day on the coast near Land's End. But nothing was discovered to tell what ship it was, where it was from, or what was the destination that it never reached.

The ship that saw the light was saved; the ship that did not was lost.

THE VANISHED LIGHTHOUSE KEEPER

The lighthouse always has two keepers, so that one is always available every night of the year. The keeper not on duty can take his ease, or work in the garden beside the house. Usually the keepers are not local people – Trinity House preferred not to employ locals, to ensure there was no favouritism. Well, not so long ago these two lighthouse keepers on St Agnes were always rowing about one thing or the other. Chalk and cheese they were. Their arguments could be heard all over the island. The one was a keen gardener and was often seen in his garden when not on duty. Unsurprisingly the other, a man with unfortunately crooked teeth, was never seen in the garden at the same time as his colleague.

Then one day the arguments ceased. The voices no longer echoed from the tower. Islanders said it was good to get some peace at last. But after a while they noticed that one of the keepers had not been seen for some days. The remaining keeper had no idea where his colleague might have gone. He carried on as best he could, tending his light every night and his garden by day. But his fellow keeper was never seen again. It was presumed that he fled unnoticed to the mainland or maybe even committed suicide. The remaining keeper ended his tour of duty shortly afterwards and left Scilly for ever. His garden became overgrown as the replacement keepers were not gardeners.

Many years later, when some buildings were being constructed nearby, as workmen were digging the old garden to lay the foundations, they found a skeleton only 3ft beneath the surface.

Some islanders thought they recognised the skeleton by its crooked teeth.

By then the other keeper was far away and probably not of this world. But it seems likely that for a while St Agnes hosted a murderer and his victim.

Jamie shuddered at the thought; Lizzie grinned. Then, returning to the foot of the tower, they headed west. As they walked they were joined by a young boatman from Tresco called Matthias Jenkin. He indicated the lighthouse.

'Did he tell you about the argumentative keepers?'

'Why yes.'

'My family heard different.'

'That's often the way with stories,' said Anthony. 'Tell us.'

SOJOURNERS

The junior lighthouse keeper was a Scotsman, James Christie; Jamesie they called him. The senior keeper was an older man, Percival Fincham. A real gentleman he was, but quiet, pale, short of stature. He kept himself to himself, but he was completely dedicated to two things: his work and his wife. He tended the light as if his life depended on it.

His wife Susannah was very different: much younger, in her mid-twenties. She was beautiful, a placid, graceful, slow-moving lady. An unusual man to be a lighthouse keeper and an unusual wife for such a man. He was besotted with her. Apparently she had married him on condition he dedicated his life to saving souls from the sea. It seemed that they both had things to hide or to hide from.

One night, despite the faithfully trimmed light, a brigantine sailing from Bristol to London was driven onto the Crim Rocks. The crew and the one passenger took to the ship's boat and morning saw them straggling ashore at Periglis. As on many times before, the islanders took them in, dried them, fed them and sent them on their way. The sole passenger was an adventurer called Negra. Passing the lighthouse cottage, he caught sight of Susannah. There was a flash of recognition between them. Before sailing for Penzance, Negra returned to the cottage.

Fincham asked him: 'How, how are you alive? I thought you were on the *Anthony*?'

'I was indeed on the *St Anthony*, en route to Oporto, fully laden and top heavy with iron. In the fog it was run down by another ship, the *Resolution*. Our ship capsized in seconds. As it went down I clung on to ropes trailing from the *Resolution* and I was pulled on board.'

'And Rozel, Felix Rozel, what of him?' asked Susannah.

'The wine merchant? He fell into the sea. The last I saw, he was clinging to a spar.'

After Negra left, Fincham and his wife talked on.

'Rozel, Rozel could be alive!'

'You are a married woman now. To you he is dead.'

'I am a dutiful wife. But perhaps we were both too hasty to dismiss the past.'

'A wife has done with lovers.'

'Perhaps you should have married the Lady Agatha after all.'

One day in the following spring a small sloop arrived at Periglis, ostensibly sheltering from contrary winds.

Fincham was in the tower. Jamesie, in the gallery, saw a man come ashore and walk briskly across the island, briefly call at the lighthouse cottage, then return.

Asking for directions or a cup of water, thought Jamesie.

As the summer passed, Fincham received many letters: from a cousin managing his lands, concerning aristocrats fleeing the French Revolution, concerning forsaken responsibilities. It was as if the past was regaining its hold on him.

Susannah spent hours gazing to seaward, watching the ships come and go.

On 12 September, a day of light winds, a ship ghosted in from the south and anchored, unremarked, in St Mary's roadstead, one of several ships in transit.

That night Jamesie was busy in the lighthouse, checking the lamps, trimming them, winding the mechanism. At midnight he was startled to hear a piercing cry. Whether of fear, anger or response, Jamesie could not guess. He shivered at the sound, but then returned to his duties and was soon engrossed, happy that at 3a.m. Fincham, always regular as clockwork, would relieve him.

But Fincham did not come. Jamesie dared not leave his post and wearily laboured on. In the morning he was called by an islander.

'They are gone. Fincham and his wife are gone.'

The cottage was empty. The ship that had anchored in the roadstead the night before was gone. The sails were just visible on the southern horizon.

'They must have left on that ship,' concluded the islander.

In time, new keepers were sent, but Jamesie knew his master's devotion to his duties – to abandon them was utterly out of character. In his mind he reviewed all that had happened. No, he thought, Fincham was not on that ship.

He was right.

THE STORY OF BIG POOL

Leaving the lighthouse, they walked down to the sandy heath around Big Pool.

'Do you know … ?' began Lizzie.

'It's the only freshwater lake in the Isles of Scilly,' chorused Jamie and Anthony together.

'How did you know that?' exclaimed Lizzie.

Once there was no sand here at all, just rock ledges and sea pools. Big Pool and Little Pool did not exist. Then on St Martin's Day, 11 November 1099, there was the highest tide anyone had ever known. Water poured across the low-lying land. The islanders ran to the high ground. When they returned, they found that sand covered everything and so it was for nearly 700 years.

Then on Saturday, 1 November 1755 there was the great All Saints Day earthquake that destroyed the city of Lisbon. There are some still alive today that remember what happened. Waves 10ft high came racing up from the south-west. The tide went out further than anyone had ever known and then three great waves swept the island. Then those waves piled up the sand even more, leaving the Big and Little Pools trapped behind it.

St Agnes took the brunt of the storm and protected St Mary's. I don't suppose anyone ever thanked them for it!

ST AGNES

Nearby, the church of St Agnes overlooked a sandy bay.

'This is Periglis,' announced Lizzie.

'Interesting,' said Anthony. 'It was probably originally called Porth Eglos, church cove. It tells us there was a church here when people spoke Cornish.'

'Who was Saint Agnes then?' chimed Jamie.

'Agnes was the daughter of a Roman noble; she was raised as a Christian. But that was the time of the Emperor Diocletian, who hated and persecuted Christians.

'Agnes had many high-ranking suitors but she turned them all down. So out of spite they reported her to the authorities for being a Christian.

'A prefect called Sempronius condemned Agnes to be dragged naked through the streets and taken to a brothel. But she prayed and by a miracle her hair grew very long and completely covered her body so no one could see it.

'In the brothel all the men that tried to take advantage of her were struck blind. Finally, the son of Sempronius joined them and he was struck dead. But then Agnes prayed for him and he came back to life, so Sempronius let her go free.

'When Diocletian heard this he was outraged and ordered Agnes to be tried again by a different prefect. This one sentenced her to death. She was tied to a stake to be burned, but the flames realised she was innocent and refused to burn her, so eventually the officer in charge cut off her head.'

'That's horrid,' said Lizzie.

'Indeed,' said Anthony. 'Persecuting anyone for their religion is not right. Persecuting someone because they won't marry you is spiteful. Jealousy is a terrible thing.'

The church was sadly dilapidated. A workman was busy making a timber frame to shore up the west wall.

'Sad, isn't it,' he said to the travellers. 'Last year's storms nearly took the roof off. Old Walter Haskin did the best he could back in 1685, but I'm afraid it won't last much longer.'

'What's to be done, parson?' asked Anthony.

'I'm not the parson, just the lay preacher. I read the homily that is sent over from St Mary's. A clergyman is provided by the SPCK, but he is shared with St Martin's, so quite often I lead the services. But as for the church, we plan to petition the governor for the proceeds of the next decent wreck. We need a stone building with good timbers for the roof and maybe a ship's bell to ring on Sundays.' He indicated a neat row of graves, lovingly tended.

'All around us is holy ground. For every ten locals planted here nine are from the Hicks family! And for every one of them there are another ten unknown sailors. There may be hundreds of them from Sir Cloudesley Shovell's fleet. They and we deserve a proper church."*

'Amen,' said Anthony.

THE GHOST OF ROSEVEAR

'I'm afraid they weren't the first and they weren't the last to be lost on the Western Rocks,' continued the lay preacher. 'The spirits of many drowned seamen still haunt the Western Rocks, in particular Rosevear, the largest of them.

'Once there was an opera singer and actress called Ann Cargill. She was a child prodigy who ran away from home and made her name in Covent Garden and Drury Lane. In 1776, aged just 16, she took the

---

*   The present church was built in 1821 with money raised by the St Agnes Pilots from the sale of a ship abandoned on the Western Rocks. The church bell was also from the ship.

lead in the famous *Beggar's Opera*. She was popular and beautiful, but her romantic life was at best colourful and at worst scandalous. She eloped several times before heading to Calcutta, India, in 1783 to be with her latest love. His name was John Haldane of Gleneagles, a ship's captain for the British East India Company. She did not know that his friends called him 'the child of misfortune'. He had captained four ships, and lost every one. Though unmarried, in India Ann became pregnant and gave birth to a son.

'This outraged the prime minister, William Pitt the Younger, who said "an actress should not be defiling the pure shores of India" and ordered that she should be sent back to Britain.

'So in 1784 Ann joined John Haldane on his packet the *Nancy* for the voyage from Bombay back to England.

'But off Scilly the *Nancy* met a terrible storm and struck the Gilstone; then she was driven east to the Rosevear Ledges, taking on water all the time. Finally, she sank in deep water near the reef.

'The crew took to the lifeboat but the waves dashed it on to the rocks of Rosevear, killing every one of them. There most of the bodies were found, including those of John Haldane and Ann Cargill, still clutching her 18-month old son.

'When the storm subsided, they were all given paupers' graves on that tiny, desolate island.

'Later, when it was realised who the victims were, their bodies were reburied on St Mary's. The burial was paid for by jewels that were found on Anne's body.

'The whole nation was shocked and soon afterwards a stranger came to Scilly. No one knew his name. He simply identified himself as "a gentleman". At his own expense a monument was made to mark Ann's final resting place. After he left the island a single rose was found on her grave.

'But near Rosevear sailors still hear a beautiful voice, a lady forever singing her last song.'

TROY TOWN MAZE

Jamie scampered ahead as they continued around the island.

'What are you lookin' for, boy?'

'A town. Badger said I had to go to the town and there I would meet Uncle Tom.'

'Well you've found them!' said the old man, 'I'm Thomas Mortimer and there is Troy Town.'

'I'm pleased to meet you, Uncle. But where is the town? All I can see are these stones on the grass.'

'Those stones are what we call Troy Town. It's a labyrinth. You often find them by the sea. This one was put here by a bored lighthouse keeper in 1792. There may have been one before that, but no one really knows. People say it's supposed to represent the city of Troy, but I don't think it's true. Who'd build a city like that?'

'What is it then?'

'I think the name is Cornish: Tretowan, place by the sand dunes. They are always made on grassy links by the sea.'

Jamie started walking the labyrinth, twisting this way and that until he reached the centre.

'Do that seven times without stopping or stumbling or crossing a wall and you'll be sure of fair winds,' said Uncle Tom. Jamie looked blank.

'The old sailors said that when you walk the maze the bad winds follow you in there, then once they are in they can't get out. By the time you're finished only the fair winds are left and it's safe to put to sea.'

'Ah, like the Boscastle witches tying up the wind in knots.'

Then it was Uncle Tom's turn to look blank.

GARLIC MILK

Then Lizzie and Anthony arrived and they made as if to continue around the island.

'Mind you shut the gate won't you?' said Uncle Tom. 'We don't need any more garlic milk.'

'Uncle Tom!' exclaimed Lizzie. 'There must be a story about garlic milk. Please tell us!'

So Uncle Tom began.

Scillonians have kept cattle since Roman times. Backalong, most families had a pig or a cow, or at least a few hens. There were small herds of cows on Tresco and St Mary's. But by the time any of the milk got as far as St Agnes it was a day old, and if the weather was bad there was no milk at all. So one day, old man Hicks at Troy Town decided that he would get some cows. He smuggled them in from Newlyn, one at a time, on his brother's fishing boat. No one else knew they was here. Nine cows he had. Good 'uns too. The milk was rich and creamy.

Well, of course, on St Mary's they wondered why all the folks from Agnes had stopped buying milk. It wasn't long before the cows were spotted from a St Mary's gig that was passing.

Then, strange to relate, one moonless night the gate to the meadow was mysteriously left open. You wouldn't have thought it was any trouble, on an island like this there's nowhere for the cattle to run to. Soon they were rounded up and the good people of Agnes could have milk in their tea once again. But then from every house came cries of horror. Everyone's tea was garlic flavoured!

You look there, beside the path, those lovely white flowers. They are St Agnes' own flower, some people call them snowbells, they grow everywhere on the island. The cows love them and given half a chance will gorge themselves on them. But the flower's other name is three-cornered garlic. It doesn't do the cows any harm, but it does mean the milk is garlic flavoured!

The lads from St Mary's, they laughed and laughed. Laughed a bit too much I reckon. I can't prove anything, but I bet it was them that rowed over to Periglis that night and opened the gate to the meadow. Ever since then this gate has been tied with twine in a special St Agnes' knot. There's precious few can tie it, even fewer can untie it and it certainly can't come undone on its own.

THE NAG'S HEAD

'Badger said I should have a drink at the Nag's Head.'

'Well you're headed the right way,' said old Tom. 'Do you have a drink with you?'

Jamie patted the leather flask at his waist.

'You'll be all right then, enjoy the walk.'

After five minutes on the downs above them they saw an amazingly weathered standing stone about 15ft high. From one side it did look a bit like a horse's head.

Lizzie grimaced, 'It was a joke, Badger was teasing us.'

'I don't think he would have done that to someone he didn't like,' said Jamie, 'We can trust him, he's a storyteller!'

ST WARNA

Their walk took them around the head of St Warna's Cove and after five minutes they reached a rocky outcrop. Beside it was a small well in the hillside with stone walls and capping. Steps inside led down to the water: it was St Warna's Well.

'I'd never heard of St Warna until today,' said Jamie.

Anthony looked thoughtful. 'We know very little about him, or more likely, her. Warna would have been a Celtic Christian, some time in the sixth to eighth centuries.'

She could have been a follower of St Bridget of Kildare or maybe St Patrick. Then she became a missionary, like Columba of Iona. Tradition says that she sailed here from Ireland in a little wicker boat, covered on the outside with hides. Another version has it that she sailed across in a wicker basket! It sounds like a traditional Irish Curragh to me. Whatever it was, this bay is named after her, either because she landed here or because she lived here.

She must have had a little cell, a hut in which to live. But there's no record of a chapel here, and although her name is preserved in the landscape, it's not the island's name as on St Martin's, St Mary's or Samson. So perhaps her influence was not so strong or lengthy.

Warna had to have a source of water, probably this spring. In time, by association with the saint, local people believed it was holy and its waters were thought to be curative.

At wells like this most communities hold a well-blessing ceremony on the saint's feast day. It's a thanksgiving: for the gift of water, for the well's properties and for the saint's ministry. It happens all over the land.

People often threw pins and other silver objects into their wells for luck, or to accompany prayers or wishes, though silver objects do have a purifying effect too. It's common all over Great Britain, just an innocent tradition or superstition, rather than anything serious.

People will still tell you that the shadowy figure of St Warna can be seen at dusk between Troytown and the Downs.

THE BEADY POOL

Beyond St Warna's cove was a prominent headland. On either side, coves with sandy beaches pinioned the granite.

The wind was in the west, so the easterly cove, Wingletang Bay, was beautifully sheltered.

Lizzie lay on the sand. Jamie scrambled over the rocks to the centre of the bay, the last part to drain. In the water he noticed something gleaming. He had found the Beady Pool.

Among the pebbles he found handfuls of beads, sea-smoothed and polished. It looked as if they were made of glass, but with terracotta on the outside.

'People say they are from a ship that was wrecked last century,' said Lizzie. 'Some say it was Dutch, others say Venetian; no one really knows.'

THE ST AGNES LOBSTER MAN

They followed the coast northwards. On their right was a cove that shone a brilliant azure in the sun. Further right was the island of Gugh and ahead they could see the sand bar that linked it to Agnes. But then from the west a band of mist rolled in from the ocean. Soon they could see only a few yards, and the moisture clung to their hair. Evening was coming in early.

'Quick,' said Lizzie. 'Get some seaweed. Tie it on your coat.'

There was urgency in her voice, so Jamie ran to the water's edge and found three good lengths of seaweed. Swiftly they continued to Abraham Hick's cottage in Higher Town.

'Welcome,' said Badger. 'Wasn't a drink at the Nag's Head good enough for you?'

'It was fine,' said Jamie.

'Oh,' Badger sounded disappointed.

'We got the seaweed,' said Lizzie. 'Just like you told me.'

'Yes, tell us about the seaweed,' said Anthony.

Badger looked embarrassed, but only for a moment. Then he told this story:

I'm not sure if this tale was invented by an islander to tease visitors, or by a visitor to tease the islanders. But you can never be too careful.

Now lobsters never stop growing. If they avoid being caught, they just get bigger and bigger. They simply shed their old shell and then grow a bigger one. If they need a new leg or claw they just grow that too. It's said that they can live for a hundred years, getting bigger all the time. Old sailors tell you they are immortal.

There was once a fisherman. He reckoned he could talk to the lobsters and they'd talk back to him. You'd hear him mumbling to himself as he went about his business. He reckoned he understood their ways and that was probably true.

Now there was one group of rocks where no other fishermen would ever go. There lived Captain Barnacle, the oldest lobster in the world, the biggest lobster in the world.

Well, this fisherman went lamp-fishing there one misty night. No one knew what happened to him. Next day his boat was found drifting off Periglis. His hat, his coat and his pipe were still lying on the thwart as if they had just been put there. But of the fisherman there was no sign at all.

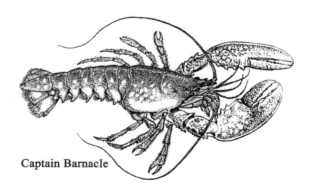

Captain Barnacle

But after that, on dark, misty nights, people started seeing a strange creature down by Periglis, heading up the lane towards Middle Town: it was half lobster, half man.

Lobsters are nocturnal; St Agnes Lobster Man is nocturnal. Lobsters are territorial; Lobster Man is never far away. Lobster Man haunts the lanes of St Agnes on misty nights.

Then the people of St Agnes wear some seaweed if they have to walk out in the darkness. Lobster's eyesight isn't good and it tells him they are one of his own, just in case he's hungry.

THE OLD WOMAN'S HOUSE

Later, as the evening drew to a close, Anthony asked Badger where they might spend the night.

'Anthony can sleep in front of the fire here,' said Badger, 'and Lizzie can have my daughter's old room. But Jamie will have to sleep in the old woman's house.'

Jamie was about to ask where to go when a quiet voice in the corner said: 'Come with me lad, I'll show you where to go.'

It was Joseph, the boatman they had met when they arrived. Jamie followed him into the starlight. He led the way to a small cottage.

'Is this the Old Woman's House?' asked Jamie.

The boatman called out, 'Old woman, old woman, are you home?'

A female voice responded, 'Who are you calling an old woman, you rascal?'

The door was opened by a definitely young woman. 'Come on in Joseph,' she said. 'Who's your young friend?'

Jamie was introduced to Annie, Joseph's wife.

'Badger just told this lad he was to sleep in the Old Woman's House, so I said I'd take him there.'

Annie laughed. 'It'll be calm enough tomorrow. There was a red sky tonight.'

Jamie looked confused.

'There's a bed for you in the back room,' said Joseph. 'We'll visit the Old Woman's House tomorrow.'

After breakfast next day Joseph led Jamie to the water's edge. On a stout mooring was Joseph's fishing boat. Soon they had left Porth Conger. North of St Agnes the little craft turned to the west, the sails now hauled close to the centreline of the boat. After a while another island appeared.

'That's Annet,' said Joseph. 'It means kittiwake in the old tongue.'

The island looked small and barren, but every rock was crammed with sea birds, with puffins prominent.

'Is the house there?' asked Jamie, increasingly worried.

'In a manner of speaking. Ready about!'

There was the flapping of sails as the boat turned south and sailed between Annet and St Agnes.

'I can see it, I can see it!' cried Jamie.

South of the island, perched on sea-washed rocks, was the cottage. But the closer they got the more puzzled Jamie became. Soon they were alongside. What in silhouette had looked like a cottage was just a mass of sea-worn granite. There was no old woman but instead a cloud of sea birds.

'That's Badger for you,' said Joseph. 'It's one of his favourite jokes. The only person that lives there is Peter Puffin! Those rocks beyond, they're called Hellwethers; beyond them are the Three Brothers.'

Jamie smiled. 'So next time I see Badger I can tell him the three brothers told me what a scoundrel he is!'

Joseph nodded, 'Badger would like that.'

THE OLD WOMAN'S HOUSE
IN RHYME*

The boat rocked with the rhythm of the waves. Joseph quietly started to speak in rhyme:

'Old woman, old woman, old woman,' said I,
''Tis a mighty queer place to be building a home,
In the teeth of the gales and the wash of the foam,
With nothing in view but the sea and the sky;
It cannot be cheerful or healthy or dry.
Why don't you go inland and rent a snug house,
With fowls in the garden and blossoming boughs,
Old woman, old woman, old woman?' said I.
'A garden have I at my hand
Beneath the green swell,
With pathways of glimmering sand
And borders of shell.
There twinkle the star-fish and there
Red jellies unfold;
The weed-banners ripple and flare
All purple and gold.

---

*   'Patlander' (Crosbie Garstin, 1887–1930) in *Punch, or the London Charivari*, Vol. 159, 15 September 1920.

And have I no poultry? Oh, come
When the Equinox lulls;
The air is a-flash and a-hum
With the tumult of gulls;
They whirl in a shimmering cloud,
Sun-bright on the breeze;
They perch on my chimneys and crowd
To nest at my knees,
And set their dun chickens to rock on the motherly
Lap of the seas.'
'Old woman, old woman, old woman,' said I,
'It sounds very well, but it cannot be right;
This must be a desolate spot of a night,
With nothing to hear but the guillemot's cry,
The sob of the surf and the wind soughing by.
Go inland and get you a cat for your knee
And gather your gossips for scandal and tea,
Old woman, old woman, old woman,' said I.
'No amber-eyed tabby may laze
And purr at my feet,
But here in the blue summer days
The seal-people meet.
They bask on my ledges and romp
In the swirl of the tides,
Old bulls in their whiskers and pomp
And sleek little brides.
Yet others come visiting me
Than grey seal or bird;
Men come in the night from the sea
And utter no word.
Wet weed clings to bosom and hair;
Their faces are drawn;
They crouch by the embers and stare
And go with the dawn
To sleep in my garden, the swell flowing over them
Like a green lawn.'

Half an hour later Jamie was scrambling ashore in Porth Conger. He returned to Higher Town to find Lizzie and Anthony still there. After a brief greeting they were startled to see Jamie march up to Badger.

'Sleep well?' enquired Badger mischievously.

'Very well,' said Jamie. 'But at the Old Woman's House I met the three brothers and they insisted I tell you what a scoundrel you are!'

For a second Badger stood, mouth agape. Then he gave the biggest laugh possible.

'Excellent!' he cried.

GUGH

'Of course,' said Badger, his eyes twinkling, 'it's considered most impolite to visit these parts without saying hello to the Old Man Cutting Turf on Gugh, and most people pay their respects at Obadiah's grave on the way there.'

'I see,' said Jamie warily. 'How old is the Old Man?'

'No one knows,' said Badger. 'At least a hundred!'

Laughing, they walked down to the sand bar between St Agnes and Gugh. The tide was going out.

'That's good,' said Lizzie, 'the currents here can be strong when the water covers the bar; it's not safe to swim and you even have to be careful wading.'

They paused at the northern crown of the island.

'It's just a heap of stones on the hillside,' said Jamie.

'With rather a small entrance,' added Lizzie, sounding disapproving.

'That's it then,' said Anthony.

'Who was Obadiah anyway?'

'Badger told me that Obadiah is the name of the local man who found this tomb. But I suspect the occupant lived between three and five thousand years ago.'

Lizzie crawled inside. Moments later there was a blood-curdling scream. Lizzie reappeared white and trembling, tears pouring down her face.

'He's in there, Obadiah, sitting up, looking at me, with great big round eye sockets. Quick, let's get away.'

Anthony gave her an avuncular hug, 'Come on, let's go and find the Old Man cutting his turf.'

THE OLD MAN CUTTING TURF

'We're in the right place, south-east of Kittern Hill, between Gull Point and Carn Kimbra, but I can't see a cottage or anything,' said Lizzie, 'Just this tall rock.'

A broad smile creased Jamie's face.

'Who told us to come here?' he asked.

'Badger, of course.'

There was a long silence. Then Lizzie stamped her foot. 'It was a joke, another of Badger's jokes. Everything Badger has ever told us is a joke AND he frightened me witless.'

The Old Man of Gugh was indeed a standing stone, magnificent, about 9ft tall, pointing roughly east.

They described the stone to Anthony, who nodded sagely, 'The tale is that there was once an old man who cared nothing for the Sabbath day. One Sunday, despite the priest's injunctions he went out turf cutting, but he never came home. Next day his neighbours went looking for him and they found he had been turned to stone.'

Suddenly something caught Lizzie's eye. A ship was rounding the Garrison and heading east.

'It's Godolphin's ketch, they are going back to Cornwall!'

Spontaneously all three cheered.

'We are safe.'

'Just a few days more and we can go home!'

'John Carter will take us back to Mullion.'

The ship rounded Peninnis and was lost to view. Light of heart, they completed their walk around the island and then set sail for St Mary's.

11

UNDEG

THE TAIL OF THE TALE

Travelling – it leaves you speechless, then turns you into a storyteller.
Ibn Battuta

ARRESTED

That night in the Union Inn, Anthony and Jamie played their fiddles.
A young man in the corner played the flute; Jamie wondered if he had
seen him before. Lizzie danced, moving naturally and gracefully to
the music. Others sang songs, told tall tales and cracked jokes. The
community had few possessions, but it was rich.

Jamie stepped outside for a breath of fresh air. The stars were bright
and the sea was quiet. The flautist joined him.

'Good evening young fiddler, James Silk-Buckingham. I'm sorry to be
nosy, but could you please explain how you got your rather good violin.'

'It was a present, sir. From a man called Joseph Emidy.'

'That explains it! I recognised the bag when I saw you in the
Benbow a couple of weeks ago. In that case we have a friend in
common. Mr Emidy gave me flute lessons in Flushing for two years.
He said he had given his old fiddle to a young violinist. I am pleased
to meet its new owner.'

Buckingham continued, 'I don't like the press gang. The way they
treated Emidy was brutish – kidnapping a musician from the opera

house and keeping him at sea for five years. So I'm pleased they didn't get you as well!'

Next day a message was sent to John Carter. Jamie started to write down their adventures so they could make them into a book. In the evening they told more stories in the Union. It seemed their troubles were over. A few days later, on 1 November, Jamie was on the quay, hoping to spot the *Phoenix*.

Suddenly he heard a shout.

'You, boy, I want to speak with you!'

It was Reverend Whitfield.

'You don't go to school or church and you were with Aunt Polly. You're a witch boy aren't you! The Constable of Penzance wants you. You're coming with me.'

Jamie was seized and dragged to the Star Castle. They were met by the Corporal of the Guard.

'Lock up this young criminal,' ordered Whitfield.

Jamie was put in a cell. But after ten minutes the door opened. In came the soldier they had met on Tresco.

'I am Lieutenant Heath,' he said. 'Please remind me of your name.'

'James Vingo James.'

'What are you doing here, Jamie? Tell me your story.'

'Which story?' asked Jamie, suddenly confident.

'Any story you wish.'

So Jamie began. With some verve he told the story of Jack the Giant Killer. As he finished the lieutenant smiled.

'You really are a storyteller aren't you? Where do you live?'

'Cury Churchtown, the Lizard.'

'Which explains why here they haven't seen you in school or in church. What about the press gang?

'It was in Penzance, I hid under the table. They went away.'

Heath smiled, 'Can anyone support your account?'

'Mr Silk-Buckingham.'

'How do you know Aunt Polly?'

'I met her by Old Town church. She was going to visit Widow Banfield and she showed me the way here.'

'I see,' said Heath. 'Do you remember the tales of the witches on Tresco?'

'Yes, the overlooked sheep.'

'And who told it?'

'Reverend Whitfield.'

'Who learned it from the farmer, who wanted to conceal that his sheep had a contagion and wanted to blame anyone else. Jamie, don't you worry, this story will end well.'

ON TRIAL

The wood-panelled office was imposing. At the head of the table sat Major Henry Bowen, Commandant and Magistrate of the Isles of Scilly. Jamie sat on one side, Rev. Whitfield on the other. Anthony was guided to a chair by the door.

Bowen began: 'Gentlemen, I have asked you here for a preliminary hearing. It may be to the advantage of all of us.'

'Reverend Whitfield, you have brought a complaint against Master James Vingo James that he is a deserter and a vagrant aiding and abetting criminal mischief and witchcraft.'

Whitfield smiled confidently. Bowen continued.

'However, evading the press gang is not desertion. Until men are pressed they are free.

'Regarding vagrancy, I'm aware of current concerns regarding itinerants, vagrants and the like. But no act has ever been passed to supplant the Vagrancy Act of 1550. Also Master James is not without fixed abode. His home is at Cury so I cannot entertain a complaint on these grounds.

'I await evidence of criminal mischief.'

Whitfield replied, 'The Constable of Penzance tells me this boy abetted a theft from his tender on Bryher five days ago.'

'A theft of what?'

'A cork.'

'A cork!'

'A cork, without which the tender would have sunk.'

'And where is the Constable of Penzance?'

'Penzance.'

'He has not sunk?'

'It appears not.'

'Where is his affidavit?'

'He entrusted me with this information …'

'Hearsay is not admissible. As for witchcraft, the Act of 1604 under which prosecutions were once made was repealed in 1735. But under the 1735 Act it is a crime to *claim* anyone is guilty of witchcraft. I advise caution lest you incriminate yourself.'

'Impossible,' snorted Whitfield. 'I claim Benefit of Clergy.'

'I am happy to refer your case to the Archdeacon's Court, but I recommend against it.'

'How so?'

'As your evidence is solely personal testimony the court will consider your character and reputation. Of course, your holy orders and master's degree will add gravity to your claims.'

Whitfield smiled.

Bowen continued: 'But I've read your book *The Isles of Scilly and its Legends*. A legend is an ancient tale preserved by a scribe or by oral tradition. But your "legends", engaging though they are, are both newly invented and misleading.'

'This is irrelevant!'

Bowen was undeterred, 'For example, "The Knight and the Dwarf" describes a fictitious event. In it you have an abbot where there was a prior. You have an abbey built like a castle, where there was just a priory the size of a parish church. You have scores of men, but the population was tiny. This, like all your "legends", is neither truth nor folk tale; it is historical fiction.'

'Wait,' frowned Whitfield. 'This is a false argument. Are you claiming that folk tales and fairy stories are true?'

Anthony James stood and all looked towards him. Somehow his sightlessness gave him great presence. 'Gentlemen, it is rare that our folk tales are literally true. They are not claimed as true and no one expects them to be true. But, like Biblical parables and Aesop's fables, they do each have a message; they have truth within them. That is why they survive.'

There was a moment of silence, then Bowen whispered, 'Reverend Whitfield, in that tale you blame a wife for the date of delivery of her child and womankind as the root of all mischance or evil. You casually mock a dwarf for his form. What will the archdeacon think of that?

'Your tales of witches read like fantasies of the Witchfinder General. Yet Lieutenant Heath has noted the good work of the ladies of Tresco in the absence of nurse, midwife or doctor. The SPCK has given Aunt Pender a pension of £5 for her service!

'Similarly, your tales of wreckers do not withstand scrutiny. The list of islanders lost attempting rescues is sobering.'

'I have just heard that no one expects such tales to be true.'

Bowen looked straight at Whitfield: 'But your record is of creating fiction and presenting it as fact. However, your claims are countered by responsible witnesses. But, as you are so keen on ecclesiastical justice I will be pleased to forward my views to the Bishop of Exeter.'

Whitfield was thoughtful. He looked hard at the proud, blind soldier and his son. He remembered Aunt Polly with her basket of provisions. He remembered the lovingly tended sailors' graves of St Agnes.

He stood, suddenly composed, an imposing figure.

'That won't be necessary,' he said. 'Jamie, I have judged you harshly and for that I am sorry. In return I hope you will judge my stories with compassion. Like your folk tales, my stories, imperfect though they may be and however you may describe them, also contain grains of truth, plucked with care from the sands of the past.'

There was a moment of silence. Then Jamie reached up and shook hands with Reverend Whitfield.

Major Bowen smiled. 'You are all free to go. Tell your tales to whoever will listen. Let time be your judge.'

Jamie ran and hugged Anthony; they held hands and walked into the sunshine.

12

DEWDHEK

SETTING SAIL

Some days later the youngsters were chatting.

'It's a shame you can't stay till Christmas. We have guising, dancing, carols, it's great fun.'

'We have those in Cury. The girls are disguised as boys and the boys as girls! We have a play of Saint George and Father Christmas. There are songs and step dancing.'

'Perhaps another time, any time. It's Gravel Night on Shrove Tuesday: we throw stones at windows and people give us pancakes; on Good Friday we float paper boats in the harbour. For May Day we have a maypole and dancing. It's bonfires and tar barrel racing at Midsummer, then Nicla Thies is our harvest home feast and dance. It's Ringing Tide on November 5th, then we start again.'

'We do lots of those,' said Jamie.

'Maybe I could come and see you.'

'Yes please.'

At the quay, the *Phoenix* was nearly ready to sail. Lizzie was a delight and Scilly was lovely, but both Anthony and Jamie looked forward to seeing Martha and little Sarah again.

'Thank you, Lizzie,' said Anthony. 'You've been a wonderful companion and guide. We are truly grateful.'

He reached out his hand and she grasped it very tight. Anthony smiled.

'Bye, bye Lizzie,' said Jamie. He handed her a small parcel.

'What is it?'

'Look and see.'

Lizzie unwrapped the present. It was a necklace, a curious assortment of beads on some fishing twine.

Lizzie blushed. 'Oh thank you.'

'It's a story necklace. One bead from the Beady Pool for each story that we have shared.'

Lizzie put it on. Like all story necklaces, it fitted perfectly.

PRINCIPAL SOURCES OF STORIES

Anon., *The Sailor's Tragedy,* Broadsheet (Stirling, W. Macnie, 1825)

Avienus, Rufus Festus, Morley, R. (tr) *Ora Maritima,* https://topostext.org/work/751, pp.114–129, 380–389, 404–415. *Himilco's Voyage*

Bottrell, W., *Traditions and Hearthside Stories of West Cornwall, Vol. 2* (Penzance, 1873) pp.31, 233, 275, 277 *Jackie's Flight*

Cooke, J.H. *The Shipwreck of Sir Cloudesley Shovell on the Scilly Islands in 1707* (Gloucester, John Bellows, 1883)

Courtney, M.A., 'Cornish Folk-Lore' in *The Folk-Lore Journal, Vol. 5, No. 1.* (London, 1887) pp.22, 38–45

Hearn, E.H. (tr) *The Sagas of Olaf Tryggvason and of Harald the Tyrant* (London, Williams and Norgate, 1911) from Storm, G., (ed.) *Heimskringla*

Heath, R., *A Natural and Historical Account of the Isles of Scilly* (London, R. Manby and H.S. Cox, 1750) *Many references especially Scilly 'aunts'*

Hunt, R., *Popular Romances of the West of England,* two volumes (London, J.C. Hotten, 1865) pp.202, 208 *Lethowsow*

'Patlander' (Crosbie Garstin) in *Punch, or the London Charivari,* Vol. 159, 15 Sep 1920 *The Old Woman's House in Rhyme*

Rawe, D.R., *Traditional Cornish Stories and Rhymes* (Padstow, Lodenek, 1971) p.45 *The Sea Bucca*

Simpson, B.J., *The Blue Cloak* (St Mary's, Fairwinds, 1995) *Ann Batten*

Shoberl, F. (ed), *Forget Me Not, a Christmas, New Year's and Birthday Present for 1831* (London, Ackerman, 1831) p.371: Woodley, G., *St Warna's Well*

Stevens, T., *The Pirate John Mucknell and the Hunt for the Wreck of the John* (Bloomington, AuthorHouse, 2011) *King's Pirate*

Strabo, Hamilton & Falconer (tr), *Geography,* (London, H.G. Bohn, 1857) *2.5.15, 3.2.9, 3.5.11, A Roman Sea-Captain Deceived*

Tiddy, E.J., *Maze of Scilly* (London, John Long, 1913) *Rivals, Marooned, Calm, Sojourners*

Whitfield, Rev. H.J., *Scilly and its Legends,* (Penzance & London, 1852) *Tolman Head, Holy Vale, Knight and the Dwarf, Wicked Dick, Tresco Witch Tales, The Dane's Grave, King Charles' Castle, Hangman's Island, Piper's Hole, St Warna*

HISTORICAL REFERENCES

Barratt, J., *Cromwell's Wars at Sea* (Barnsley, Pen & Sword, 2006)

Borlase, W., *Antiquities, Historical and Monumental, of the County of Cornwall* (London, W. Bowyer and J. Nichols, 1769)

Borlase, W., *Observations on the ancient and present state of the islands of Scilly* (Oxford, W. Jackson, 1754)

Boscowitz, A., *Earthquakes* (Routledge, 1890)

Bowley, R.L. and E.L., *The Fortunate Islands: a history of the Isles of Scilly* (Scilly Isles, Bowley Publications, 1964)

Carew, R., *Survey of Cornwall, 1602* (London, 1710) p.6

Courtney, J.S., *A Guide to Penzance and Its Neighbourhood: Including the Islands of Scilly* (E. Rowe, 1845)

Diodorus Siculus, *Bibliotheca Historica* Oldfather (tr), Henderson (ed) (Cambridge, Mass., Harvard, 1933) *V. 21, 22, 38*

Forester, T., *Florence of Worcester's Chronicle, (446–1295)* (London, Henry G. Bohn, 1854)

Giles, J.A., *Wm of Malmesbury's Chronicle* (Bohn, 1847) p.134

Halliwell, J.O., *Rambles in West Cornwall* (J.R. Smith, 1861) p.221 et seq

Harris, J.H., *Cornish Saints and Sinners* (London, J. Lane, 1907)

Herodotus, *Histories,* Macaulay (tr) (London, Macmillan, 1890) 3.115

Hitchins, F. and Drew, S., *History of Cornwall,* (Helston, Penaluna, 1824)

Holmes, T.R., *Ancient Britain and the Invasions of Julius Caesar* (Oxford: The Clarendon Press, 1907) p.512

Knight, C., *Popular History of England* (Knight, 1859) Vol. 5, p.334

Leyland, J., *The Itinerary of John Leland the Antiquary, 1538–43* (Oxford, 1711) v3, 7–9

Lysons, D. and S., *Magna Britannia: Vol. 3, Cornwall.* (London, T. Cadell and W. Davies, 1814) pp.330–337

Malory, T., *Le Morte d'Arthur* (Caxton, 1485) Book 5

Matthews, G.F., *The Isles of Scilly* (London, G. Ronald, 1960)

Mothersole, J., *The Isles of Scilly: their story, their folk & their flowers.* (London, The Religious Tract Society, 1910) p.19

Mumford, C. (ed.) *The Scillonian Magazine* (Hugh Town, 1925 onwards)

North, I.W., *A Week in the Isles of Scilly* (Rowe, 1850) pp.4–7

Palgrave, F., (ed.) *Rotuli Curiae Regis, 1194–1199* (Record Comm, 1835)

Pearce, C., *Cornish Wrecking 1700–1860* (Woodbridge, Boydell & Brewer, 2010)

Pliny the Elder, *Natural History Holland (tr)* (London, Wernerian, 1847) ii. 67, 167, iv. 119, vii. 197, xxxiv. 156–158

Polwhele, R., *The History of Cornwall Vol. 3* (London, Law & Whittaker, 1816)

Silk-Buckingham, J,. *Autobiography* (London, 1855) pp.174–177

Smith, Rev. G.C., *The Scilly Islands and the Famine* (London, W.K. Wakefield, 1828)

Taunton, W.P., *Reports of Cases Argued and Determined in the Court of Common Pleas* Vol. 1, (London, 1810) p.327

Thiselton-Dyer, T.F., *British Popular Customs* (George Bell & Sons, 1876)

Thomas, C., *Exploration of a Drowned Landscape* (London, Batsford, 1985)

Tonkin, J.C., *Guide to the Isles of Scilly* (1887)

Trewin, J.C., *Up From the Lizard* (London, Carroll & Nicholson, 1948) pp.261–262

Troutbeck, Rev. J., *A Survey of the … Scilly Islands,* (London, 1796)

Weatherhill, C., *Cornish Place Names and Language* (Wilmslow, Sigma, 1999) from p.169

William of Worcester, Harvey, J., (ed.) *Itineraries,* (Oxford, Clarendon, 1969) p.25

Woodley, G., *A View of the Present State of the Scilly Islands* (Truro, 1822)